THE GIFT OF POWER

THE MACMILLAN COMPANY
NEW YORK · CHICAGO
DALLAS · ATLANTA · SAN FRANCISCO
LONDON · MANILA

In ·Canada
BRETT-MACMILLAN LTD.
GALT, ONTARIO

THE GIFT OF POWER

BY

Lewis Joseph Sherrill

New York

THE MACMILLAN COMPANY

1961

To

Thomas Sherrill Durham
John Richard Durham
and
Mary Sherrill Durham

Contents

Preface

As MAN has begun to unlock the secrets of the universe, incredible power has been given him to dispose of as he will. But it is everywhere recognized that he is not ready for the gift of power which has been put into his keeping. Not only is he unready; he is badly frightened. In this state of things he is asking some of the most searching questions which he has put to his world since the days of the Greek philosophers and the Hebrew seers.

Some of his questions are taking this general shape: Is it possible for man to become the kind of creature who can peacefully and constructively manage the power given him? Is it possible for him not only to survive but to thrive under the pressures of modern life? Or, on the contrary, is the modern world with its pressures and its dangers too much for man with his archaic equipment for a world which no longer exists? Is the human race girding itself for a final act of self-destruction? Are we now witnessing the last stages of the disintegration of man and his civilization? These are some of the terrifying questions now heard on every hand, and children as well as adults ask them.

Religion is never so relevant as when men stand thus at the parting of the ways. Indeed, nothing ultimately is so relevant to our situation today as is the central message of the Christian religion. In the conviction that this is so, this book affirms a central thesis, and inquires into three central questions.

The thesis is this: The Christian religion can teach men how to receive a gift of interior, spiritual power sufficient to enable them to cope with the gift of exterior, physical power which has been granted. The nature of this power is well expressed in the phrase *"the power to become."* In its simplest terms this means that the power which can be received is the power to become a self who can cope with itself in the modern world, and with the world in which we must live.

The three chief questions are these: Why is man so profoundly disturbed today? In what way is the Christian religion relevant to this condition? If the Christian religion is really relevant to the deeper needs of our own time, how can the church's educational work be made equally relevant?

Each of these three questions has been treated many times and by many persons, but the three need now to be brought freshly into focus as one total question. That attempt is made in this book.

As the question regarding man's plight today is pushed to deeper levels, it becomes evident that at bottom this is a religious question. That fact is now widely understood, and we are witnessing a renewal of religious concern.

The second question, regarding the relevance of Christian faith to man's predicament, is the subject of fresh exploration in many parts of the Western world. We witness a renewed concern for Biblical and theological studies, a concern so serious that not a few among the youth of the time are deserting other studies for these.

As for the educational work of the church, it received a strong new impetus during the earlier part of the twentieth century, and brilliant contributions were made. But the landscape of the world and the climate of feeling have been radically altered since the first three decades of the century, and much of the literature which served its own day well has now come to seem remote.

Meanwhile in the midst of the twentieth century a fresh awakening in the educational work of the church is beginning. The seriousness of man's plight in the modern world, and the new currents of Biblical and theological thought, are registering their impact on the educational enterprise. To this must be added the fact that the advance in psychological studies gives us a picture of man which is very different from the one that governed the writers of the classic modern works on Christian education. And as if this were still not enough, modern work in psychotherapy is yielding insights which must be incorporated into the theory and practice of Christian education.

In short, a new philosophy of Christian education is emerging as a result of the plight of modern man, and the new currents of religious and psychological thought concerning it. This book is intended as a contribution to that new philosophy of Christian education which is taking shape.

In broadest outline the sequence of thought is this: Chapters I and II are concerned with the nature of the self, and the grounds of man's anxiety. Chapter III is concerned with the Christian community as a worshiping community, where God confronts man and persons interact with one another. Chapters IV to VIII are concerned with the nature of Christian education, the relation between revelation and education, and the dynamics of interaction in the Christian community as men respond to revelation.

Two convictions, implicit throughout the book, should be made explicit at the outset. One is that the new philosophy of Christian education must come to the subject of education from within the Jewish-Christian tradition, not from outside it. More specifically, it must draw its inspiration from the peculiar genius of the Christian community and of Christian faith rather than from any form of secular society or secular education. This does not mean that we have nothing to learn from such sources. On the contrary, very much is to be learned, and we shall repeatedly acknowledge the debt. But in the end the unique nature of Christian education derives from the unique nature of the Christian community and Christian faith. This is the principal reason that, in the pages that follow, so much attention is given to the subject of revelation.

A second conviction which should be made explicit at the beginning is this: The Christian community as a whole is meant to be the scene of a redemptive ministry to the human self as a whole. To hold this view means trying to abandon two fragmentations: fragmenting the self, and fragmenting the ministries which the Christian community renders to persons.

Accordingly, on the one hand it is the needs of the human self as a total self, that we endeavor to keep constantly in sight. This is the reason for beginning with a consideration of the nature of selfhood, and the grounds of man's anxiety. And on the other hand we endeavor to treat the ministry of the Christian community to the human self as a total ministry. This is the reason that we shall have so much to say concerning interaction between persons, and the changes that take place in persons.

Much of what is said, then, is quite as relevant to preaching, to the conduct of worship, to pastoral care, counseling, administration, evangelism, missionary work, and social outreach as it is to Christian education. For in a total ministry to the total self, any sharp line of distinction between Christian education and other functions of the church grows dim and tends to disappear in the interest of wholeness in the ministry to the self, and a ministry to the wholeness of the self.

If there can be a philosophy of wholeness in the ministration of the Christian community, as well as of wholeness in the self, we believe that the new philosophy of Christian education will show a greatly lessened anxiety to prove its importance in the household of faith, and a heightened concern to participate in the total ministry of the Christian community to the total self of man.

*   *   *

The substance of the material in this book was delivered as the Robert F. Jones Lectures in Christian Education in the Austin Presbyterian Theological Seminary at Austin, Texas, in 1952. I wish to thank the students and faculty of that institution, especially President and Mrs. David L. Stitt, and Professor and Mrs. C. Ellis Nelson, for the numberless thoughtful acts which made this visit so great a personal pleasure. Nor can I forget the satisfaction of talking repeatedly with Dr. and Mrs. Robert F. Jones, in whose honor the Lectureship is named.

The substance of the material in this book was delivered on the Annual Departmental Lectureship in the School of Religion of Butler University, Indianapolis, Indiana, in 1952. I recall with a feeling of warmth the kindnesses constantly shown by the students and faculty of that school, especially by Dean Orman Shelton and Professor J. B. Miller.

Parts of the material in the book were delivered as the McFadin Lectures in Texas Christian University at Fort Worth, Texas, early in 1955. I wish to express to President McGruder E. Sadler my appreciation of the invitation to give these lectures; and to the students and faculty of Brite College of the Bible of Texas Christian University, my sense of gratitude for their warm hospitality.

A stimulating interchange of thought concerning the nature of Christian education has been going on with my colleagues in this faculty, with many interested persons in other places, and with several generations of theological students. By their support of the effort to find Biblical and theological foundations for Christian education, and by their healthy criticism of detailed ventures in that direction, they have put me under lasting obligation which I gladly acknowledge.

I have a sense of special indebtedness to Charles H. Johnson, at present a member of the faculty of Perkins School of Theology, Southern Methodist University, Dallas, Texas, who assisted me for three years in courses. Jointly we prepared materials in which much that is presented in this book was submitted to the test of critical examination by young, vigorous, devoted minds.

In the Department of Religious Education and Psychology of Union Theological Seminary my colleagues Frank W. Herriott and Mary Anderson Tully and I have found ourselves in an exciting intellectual and spiritual adventure as we have sought to explore together some of the dimensions of the new Christian education which is emerging in the midst of this fateful twentieth century. For all that I have learned from them I am profoundly grateful. I am obligated to them for reading this manuscript as well as earlier material on which it is based, and for specific suggestions, but I must not assume that they would affirm the particular propositions which are put forward in this book.

To the publishers who gave permission to quote copyrighted materials, I express cordial thanks. Specifically these are Charles

Scribner's Sons, The Ronald Press Company, Harper & Brothers, W. W. Norton & Company, and The Macmillan Company, all of New York City. Each such permission is acknowledged in the notes at the back of the book.

To my secretary, Dorothy Hollis Kalaidjian, I express appreciation for skillful assistance, unfailingly rendered in a spirit which adds greatly to the satisfaction of each day's work.

To Carolyn Lockwood O'Connor, who became my secretary while the book was in press, I am indebted for the insight with which she immediately took up the chief responsibility for reading the proof and making the index.

To Frank W. Herriott, and to Alice Lake Herriott, his wife, Mrs. Sherrill and I owe a debt of gratitude in connection with this book, as in so many other ways, which it will be impossible ever to repay. For two summers they generously put their delightful farm home at our disposal. At Sycamore Hill, which is truly a house of peace, nearly all of the final writing was done. I could hope that the serenity of days spent in such a place has left some timeless quality in what was put into words there.

My wife, Helen Hardwicke Sherrill, has given assistance in uncounted ways during the preparation of this work. But beyond all aid in specific tasks there is a deeper giving of self which inspires each undertaking and illumines the meaning of life itself.

LEWIS J. SHERRILL

UNION THEOLOGICAL SEMINARY
New York, New York
February 22, 1955

THE GIFT OF POWER

CHAPTER I

The Human Self

WHAT MAN HAS lost today is himself. He is his own lost continent. Until he finds himself, all else is lost. But his plight is twice compounded, for he can find no place to stand on so that he can search for himself.

When we say that a man is trying to find himself, we have made a strange kind of statement. Think of some of the implications which lie in such an assertion.

We imply that something immensely important to that man is going on within him, and we imply that we have a fellow feeling with him; for perhaps we, too, have trodden that same road, or we may still be treading it now. Perhaps, though, we are impatient with the other man for not getting over it sooner.

We imply that such a man is the subject in the search, that he is the one doing the thinking, feeling, and acting as this attempt is carried on. But at the same time we imply also that he is the object of his own concern. In some respects this is the strangest aspect in all this strange search: that a man should seek to find what he already is; not only to find out what he is, for that yields him merely a body of information about himself; but to find *himself*, thus connecting and welding the subject and the object, the searcher and the sought, into one so that a man can say he is "sure of himself."

We imply further that when a man is seeking to find himself he harbors some degree of doubt about himself. If he can be frank, and if he is able to put his feeling into words, he may be able to say, "I do not know who I am," or, "I do not know where I belong."[1] But the feeling of doubt concerning himself may be so vague that he is not able to define it and express it, as when he says, "I don't know what's the matter with me." In that event he may not know what he is seeking, much less how to know when he has found it.

We thus imply that until he has reached some measure of certainty regarding himself he is groping, somewhat as if he had been maimed and rendered incapable of taking his full part in life. He then may say such things as, "I feel like I am in a blind alley," or, "I can't seem to be able to get going."

When we ask what it means to say that a man is trying to find himself, we have to ask, "What is the human self?" and, "What are the threats to selfhood?" To the first of these we turn in the present chapter, and to the second of them in the next chapter. What, then, is the human self?

MARKS OF A SELF

The first mark of a self is vitality. We know this vitality at first-hand only in connection with a body. Hence it can be said that the self is a living body. The body can be examined, defined, described, recognized. But vitality can be defined only in terms of itself, that is, of life. Thus we can say that a particular body is alive, hence has vitality; or else we can say that the life of the body has ended, that vitality has left the body.

As a living body the self is a totality. It includes both the physiological and the psychological in one total. In its physiology it includes all the various systems that go to make up the body. In its psychology it includes both the conscious and the unconscious processes which characterize us as human beings.

This self which is a total living body has its own native constitution. This comprises his own particular equipment for living, an equipment peculiar to himself. This native equipment in turn both opens the possibilities of, and sets limits upon, his own development.

If the first mark of a self is life in a body, it must then be said that one is a self at the moment of one's birth. This is of course a limited meaning of the term "self," for in respect of other marks of selfhood the newborn still has to become a self. But by employing the term "self" to designate the human creature from the moment he is separated from his mother, we do three further things. We recognize him as a human being from the outset of separated life. We recognize continuity of being throughout all the vicissitudes of his becoming. And we put up a guard against the kind of thinking which assumes that we can manipulate him for his own good while he is still very young.

Furthermore, when we regard the self as the totality of a living body we discover that we can move back and forth much more readily between two types of literature concerning man which have much more in common than is generally supposed. One of these is the literature of modern medicine, psychiatry, and psychology. In that literature the unity of the body in all its functions and processes is commonly assumed. The terms "psychosomatic" and "somatopsychic" have come into general use to designate the interaction between *psyche,* or soul, and *soma,* or body; while the term "self" seems to be coming into more frequent use to designate this living totality, and a new literature called "self psychology" is springing up.[2]

The other type of literature is that which is contained in the Bible. One may well be dubious concerning any attempt to make the Bible support current thought or vice versa. But when all due caution against seeking a scientific description of man in the Bible is kept in mind, it still remains true that the Bible describes revelation to man, and redemption as redemption of man. Hence the Biblical assumptions regarding the constitution of man are not only relevant but necessary if one would attempt to stand within the Bible to grasp and be grasped by what is being said there.

No one can read the Bible attentively without being impressed by the prominent place given to the body, either the body as a whole, or to its parts, which are often called "members," and to its health, its protection, and eventually its redemption. The church is called "the body of Christ," and persons are its "members." Moreover the common habit of separating body and soul has resulted in a lost sense of the Biblical meaning of *soul*. This has then betrayed many people into a vast vagueness in speaking of the salvation of the soul. This lost sense of what the soul is may be responsible in no small part for the separation of religion from life in many of the very quarters where the Bible is most highly revered.

In the Bible the soul (*nephesh* in Hebrew, *psyche* in Greek) is the animating principle of the body. That is to say, *the soul is the life*. In Hebrew thought life has been breathed into man by God, and man has become a living soul.[3] In another way of referring to the soul, "the soul is in the blood."[4] In the New Testament *psyche* can often be translated either "soul" or "life," at choice. Thus when Jesus speaks of a man's concern over his own *psyche*, he refers to this animating principle, or vitality, which can be translated either as "soul" or as "life."[5]

The Bible has no word which corresponds exactly to the English noun "self." It is significant, however, that either of the Biblical words "soul" or "body" is an approximate equivalent of "self." Thus "soul," *nephesh* in the Old Testament or *psyche* in the New Testament, can often be translated by "self" as well as, or better than, by any other English word.

But in New Testament usage much is to be said for taking "body," the *soma*, as the equivalent of "self," especially in Paul's vocabulary. Whenever "body" is taken as generally equivalent to "self," it is to be understood that "body" refers to a living totality which functions through all its parts or "members." For in both the Old and the New Testaments what we now call psychological processes are assumed to be localized in various parts of the body, such as heart, diaphragm, kidneys, womb, and bowels.

As for Paul's usage, when he speaks of redemption it is the *body* which is to be redeemed. This is true when he thinks of redemption as a possibility open to us in the present.[6] And when he comes to speak of the resurrection, one of his greatest concerns is the kind of body one will have then and thereafter.[7] For the Platonic notion of a disembodied soul seems to have been unthinkable for Paul. In other words, the continuing identity of life in a body which we now designate by the word "self" is what Paul projects over and across the chasm of death, still seeing the self as housed in a body, albeit a new kind of body.[8]

SELF-DETERMINATION

A second mark of the self is self-determination, or will. Some prefer to distinguish between ontological will and psychological will. Ontological will is the self's determination to continue, or not to continue, in being. This would appear to be the most elemental form of will, a total response of the total being to the totality of all which confronts him. The common name for it is "the will to live."

As long as the will to live persists, the self seems able to endure either of two great extremes. One is excessive battering by hardships, disappointments, losses, defeats, and all the rest of the "slings and arrows of outrageous fortune" which befall some persons who nevertheless live on. The other extreme is the vacuumized existence which seems to an outsider to contain nothing worth living for, but where the person in question centers his life in some tiny orbit, and lives on, much like the prisoner who occupies himself with winning and taming a mouse. To all such persons as live on under whatever extremes, common speech pays tribute in sayings which are a mixture of admiration, wonder, and amusement; such as "Nothing gets him down" or "He lives on in spite of himself."

But in proportion as the will to live weakens, the self may succumb to death when it would appear to an outsider that he has everything to live for. Thoughtful physicians sometimes say of such a person, "He just decided to die," even though his death is attributed to "natural causes." And perhaps there are deaths by suicide which will yield no better explanation. As it was succinctly put in a note by a young woman who destroyed herself: "I have everything to live for but I do not have the strength to go on." And what appears to be a cessation of the will to live is sometimes seen in the case of infants who are deprived of closeness to any person. Even though they are otherwise well handled and fed with scientific correctness, they may refuse to eat.

Psychological self-determination is the determination *by the self* of its own responses to that which confronts it from without, or to tensions that arise within the self. The point of emphasis in such a statement is that the determination is from within the self.

In a very rudimentary form self-determination appears within the first few hours of life, as in accepting or rejecting food, responding to handling, and the like. It shows up a few months later in the response to persons, to toys, and other objects. It is especially noticeable in the response to suggestion. To some suggestions a child may readily respond; others leave him unmoved; while to still others he may answer with a vivid drama of screaming refusal. And as he learns to talk, one of the words he quickly captures and puts to work is "No." Few forms of human communication are any more unmistakable than a child's "No!"

In the choice between the "Yes" and the "No" in response to a person making a suggestion, we have what may be regarded as one of the earliest exercises of psychological will at a level distinctly above its rudimentary stage. For this represents the conscious facing of a relatively simple alternative and the choice within the self of the response he will make.

As age advances the alternatives become more complicated, and deciding how to respond may grow correspondingly more difficult. Many stand ready to direct the self into this or that action or course of life. But the right to say "No!" is a sort of final bastion of protection of the self's integrity against being invaded by those persons and forces standing ready to govern one's life for him.

The chief point to observe here is that from the beginning of life, but in different ways as age and experience, the self strives to protect its integrity by determining its activity from within. And in so doing, one is "de-termining" himself, that is, establishing limits around what he will or will not "willingly" do or permit to be done to him.

At the same time he is also de-termining other selves. He is finding out what other individuals feel or do not feel toward him, what they will or will not do, what they will permit or not permit, in their relationships with him. Thus by the exercise of will he is defining himself, defining other persons, and defining his relationships with them. For defining is establishing boundaries within which one can operate with a reasonable degree of certainty.

This is why the will is so basic in selfhood. This is why the experience of saying a genuine "No" is so important in the growth of a self. For both unlimited freedom and the use of coercion take away the self's right to say "No," and this in turn means the undermining of selfhood. This, too, is why restoring true freedom of choice may mark the beginning of reestablishing boundaries around a self from within the self at a time when selfhood is in danger of being lost either in the confusing fog of unlimited freedom or under the strangling effects of coercion.

For such reasons, too, the "No," especially when expressed in the form of doubt, may open the way to a deeper encounter with God. For in the relation with God, as in the relation with other human selves, the "Yes" is not a fully valid act of the self unless the "No" is genuinely possible. And it often turns out that the deeper "Yes" is possible only after the self has validated its freedom by saying "No."

SELF-CONSCIOUSNESS

A third mark of selfhood is self-consciousness, that is, the consciousness of being a self. In the course of a few months of life, say between the ages of two and three, a child commonly begins to cease referring to himself as an object, such as "Baby" or "Bill," and begins to say "I." The time when a child begins to say "I" represents the dawning of *self*-consciousness. This is regarded by many as being the time when selfhood in its proper sense begins. It seems preferable, however, to regard it as approximately the time when one begins to be *conscious of being a self*.

When a child cannot only speak but can say "I," he has definitely transcended other creatures of the animal world. There is much indeed that he has in common with them. Both he and they are enmeshed in nature. Both he and they enjoy many of the same kinds of satisfaction, and are exposed to the same kinds of hazards. They, too, have vitality. Perhaps in a limited sense they, too, have will. They, too, can communicate with one another. But in communicating they cannot say "I" as he can. In learning to use human speech, and in speaking to say "I," he has begun to claim his distinctively *human* birthright, thus taking one of his crucial steps toward becoming what it is in him to become.

The transition that here takes place in a child seems so much a matter of course that we may easily miss its great significance. It is a transition *away from* referring to himself from the outside, as other persons must do when they speak to him or speak about him. And it is a transition *toward* stating himself from within as "I." It is a transition from knowing himself as an object-to-other-persons, to knowing himself as a subject-within-himself.

And each time this transition occurs in another child, it attests that two wonders have come to pass again. One is the wonder of human speech. For of course a child is learning to speak when he can say "I." And in learning to speak he is learning to communicate through speech with others of his kind. Thus he is making his first faltering way out into the vast world of communication through uttered and written words.

This "universe of discourse," as it has long been called, is a world wherein words may serve to reveal one self to another self either when they face each other or even across otherwise unbridgeable chasms of time and space. But it is a world where on the other hand words may serve to conceal one self from another, thus creating a gulf between them even though they have been knit together.

The other corresponding wonder is that he is becoming aware that *he* is a self among selves in this drama of interacting selves. As yet he has not defined his role, although the makings of it were in him long before he began to talk. Much less does he know as yet how vast the drama is. But as a living creature who can say "I" he affirms himself as a self in the presence of other selves. He knows himself as a being who is *conscious of being*.

It goes without saying that no child puts it to himself in this way. Nor does he have any need to do so, since this simply is something that *is*. For knowing oneself as a self is a complete act of knowledge. In this act the knower, the knowing, the known, and the certainty of knowing are intertwined together and affirmed by saying "I." And no one has to teach the self that this is so unless the relationships which the self sustains to others have undermined his certainty of his own identity.

If the self *has* this certainty of itself as a self, certainty in regard to other forms and aspects of reality can be reared upon this foundation and can radiate in all directions. But in proportion as the self's certainty of itself as a self is undermined, doubt tends to radiate in all directions. Deluding and damaging "certainties" may be found inside or outside the self. Absolutes of some kind may be sought outside the self to which the self can attach itself for safety.

In the event that the consciousness of being a self is undermined, certainty concerning the reality which is outside him as well as that which is within him can be established only by establishing his certainty of himself. This in turn can be done only in relationship with at least one other self who is completely trusted.

This principle, that certainty of selfhood is established in relationship with other selves and may be reestablished in a relationship when undermined or lost, lies at the root of revelation, redemption, grace, education, counseling, and psychotherapy as well. Each in its own setting puts this life-restoring principle to work.

SELF-TRANSCENDENCE

A fourth mark of the self is self-transcendence. Consider such common expressions as "I do not understand myself," or "I think I am a pretty good sort," or any other of a host of those reflexive forms of speech which indicate that a person has caught himself in the act of looking at himself, thinking something about himself, feeling something toward himself. This way of speaking commonly begins not long after a child commences to say "I." For example, a child of less than three years of age, sitting in front of a fire, was asked, "Are you hot?" Putting his hand on his chest he replied, "Yes, I can feel myself, and know I'm hot."

This kind of thinking or speaking is even more distinctively human than is the ability to say "I." For now the human creature, in one and the same body, is both subject and object *within himself*. When he first begins to speak he apparently knows himself as an object-to-other-selves. In learning to say "I," he is becoming a subject-within-himself. But in learning to refer to himself in the objective case, as it is aptly called, he becomes object-to-his-own-self.

And if he should say, "I am trying to find myself," he is both the seeker and the sought. If he should say, "I do not understand myself," he is taking a short and better way of saying that he is a knower who knows that he does not know himself; and yet at the same time that he is an object unknown to himself as a potential knower; and that therefore and to that degree he is a mystery to himself.

In such an inward situation he is an "I" who can feel, think, act. Yet he is also a "me" whom he can feel toward, think of, speak to, do things to. As it is now often expressed, he can stand above himself and look at himself. This is self-transcendence.

Self-transcendence has at least two aspects which are of especial importance in the line of thought we are following. For one thing, self-transcendence means that the human creature, who is in nature and subject to nature, is able also at the same time to transcend nature. He dwells in the finite world of nature which cradles him. And yet he dwells also in a realm of spirit.

The realm of spirit is itself a realm which transcends physical nature in the sense that it is made up of intangibles. For while we live rooted in physical nature and dependent upon it, we are equally and perhaps even more dependent upon intangibles which, as far as can be discerned, have no physical existence. But for a given self these intangibles *do* exist. They can come and go, shrink or grow in importance, be found and be lost. The self may pine for the want of them, or suffer when he faces them, or exult when he possesses them or when they lay hold on him.

The realm of spirit contains such intangibles and imponderables as meanings and values; inductions, abstractions, and deductions; concepts such as those of justice, equality, liberty, democracy, righteousness, love and hate, decency and fair play, and a great number of others which correspond to no physical entities. The question of the kind of reality which they embody has, of course, been a battleground in philosophy, and that struggle is one of the most fascinating episodes in the long history of human thought.

Here we need only point out that intangibles of this kind are the product of human thought. They correspond to no configuration of physical matter and are not themselves made up of physical stuff. Yet they can and do pass from one self to another self. They can excite to action and aspiration, or else to such opposites as discontent, paralysis of action, despair; or else again to that middle ground of wistful longing and waiting.

We do not have to believe with Plato that goodness, beauty, truth, and other such great ideals are absolutes, although we may well enough admire *him* and the product of his great mind. But we do have to recognize that as intangibles, whatever one may decide as to their ultimate nature, they are a dynamic kind of entity which incites men both to war and to peace. This is why so many leaders of men have been able to rally other men at the call of a single great idea which spoke to their condition and told them there was hope.

But there is another kind of intangible which in some respects is even more important. This is the unique constellation of all that is within a self, which makes each particular self exactly what it is. Usage tends now to call this unique constellation a man's personality, or his character. But what we have in view now is more than the shape, posture, and interplay of all that is within him, although it includes that. We have in view also the *manifestation*, the showing forth, and the going forth, of the unique totality of a particular self.

As such it can be known by other selves even though the most painstakingly careful dissection of the body could yield no more than the most fragmentary clues as to why this person is just what he is. It is intangible and imponderable. And yet at one and the same time it has arisen out of something *within* him, it is a forthgoing of something *from* him, it can make an impact upon others, it can penetrate into other selves, and it can begin, as it were, to create its own kind within other selves.

The simplest word by which to designate this intangible "something" is *spirit*. This is the most apt of all words for the purpose, since the term *spirit* has been built up out of the basic idea of breath or wind, and readily lends itself to descriptions of what is breathed forth or wafted toward another, or what is taken in from another. For spirit is the intangible totality which the self is, and at the same time is the forth-going of that intangible totality toward and into others.

Such statements as we have just been making are readily recognizable in human experience as selves make their impact on one another. It is not surprising then that those who spoke the Hebrew, the Greek, and the Latin languages should have seized upon the words *ruach*, *pneuma*, and *spiritus*, each having to do with breath or wind in its respective language, as being among the least corporeal words, and should gradually have purged these words of all corporeality.

But they kept the sense of *real being* in the word *spirit*. And they kept as well the idea of spirit as *forth-going of real being*. Thus by the use of the term *spirit* they could designate an aspect of man's being and nature which corresponds to an aspect of God's being and nature, so making communication between them possible through a medium common to both. Then in turn it could also be better grasped that God is within man yet not identical with him. He is unutterably beyond man, and yet not separated from man by an absolute otherness.

This aspect of self-transcendence; namely, that man is in nature and yet transcends nature, has been of great value in a period when man was in grave danger of coming to regard himself as the helpless, insignificant slave of the very laws and processes of physical nature which he himself has discovered and stated.[9]

In the second place man's capacity for self-transcendence has quite a different aspect which must also be seen. This capacity means that there is always at least a potential rift in the self. This rift is more complicated than we have as yet suggested. As we have seen, in being able to stand above himself and look at himself, the self is both "I" and "me," both subject and object, both the valuer and the one being valued, the judge and the one being judged. But there may be *a rift in the subject as well*, that is, in the "I" who is doing the valuing and judging.

For when the self finds, as it must, that there are incompatible standards outside him in the environing world, and incompatible standards within himself as well, he then stands facing the question of authority. It may come in so relatively simple a form as a child's asking, "Why must I do this if I don't want to?" or it may reach proportions such as those of Newman's long struggle with the question whether he would leave the Church of England and enter the Church of Rome. But in any case as long as the "I" is divided against itself in trying to come to a state of peace over its own feelings and doings, just so long there is a rift in the subject as well as between the subject and the object.

Thus we have always to reckon with the nature of one's relationship to himself, and with the structure and functioning of his self-regard. The feeling toward one's self is a crucial factor in the self. But there is not only the question of what he feels about himself; there is the question also of why he holds such feeling and why it is so strong or so weak. The reasons are commonly found to lie far beneath the surface, down where logical arguments about moral conduct and the nature of authority simply do not penetrate.

This being so, the ideas of acceptance and self-acceptance have come to play a large part in modern theology and psychotherapy.[10] Acceptance has a healing power. It derives this power from the fact that when the self exists in a conflictual, self-doubting, guilt-ridden state of estrangement from itself, it needs first to be accepted in a relationship with another self, accepted just as it is, before that self can begin to accept itself. Then it can begin from within to become what as yet it is not but might be. The rifts in the self can begin to heal, and the self can be reunited with itself.

Seeing then that self-transcendence has this double quality of introducing us into a spiritual realm and yet of introducing rifts into the self, it is not to be wondered at that men of so many races and so many times have understood that to be a human creature means facing both glory and shame. For if the choice between good and evil were a simple choice, to be human would be simple. But men have long understood that the rift in themselves is so deep that to be human is to be exposed to tragedy such as no subhuman creature could ever know. For, being human, man can undertake to straddle the rift that is within him, and claim the incompatible goods that lie on both sides of it. To do this is called selling the soul. And we can know it is tragedy only because we are spiritual beings.

How this tragedy can be overcome and surmounted is the central theme in revelation. That it *can* be overcome is the triumphant note in the Christian gospel. Therefore such a man as Paul, who knew well enough what these cleavages in the self are, when taking the long view of a man's life in the spirit could say that we

in which this self-consciousness is related to the desire for objective truth, he writes:

Augustine knows that by nature man desires and wills, sins and repents, hopes and fears, but he never forgets that man also thinks and reasons, and that his thought is sustained by a profound interior passion for objective truth, not merely for the objectivity of natural science, but also for the ultimate objectivity of metaphysics and religious worship, which is one of our most uniquely human characteristics, something without which man would not be man as we know him in his self-consciousness and history. We have not plumbed our self-consciousness to its depths until we have discovered, at the very heart of it, our responsibility to the Other, who transcends our self-consciousness and yet is known in our self-consciousness, whose existence self-consciousness apprehends and whose nature it partly discerns by analogy with its own most intense and profound experiences.[13]

A second reason for the primary importance of self-consciousness is that it opens the way for true firsthand knowledge of God. This statement has already been partially anticipated. The statement itself can be elaborated in several possible directions, depending on the philosophical basis upon which it is further developed.

For example, it can be said that man, as a being, participates in Being-Itself, which is God. Therefore to the extent that a man truly knows himself, he truly knows God, although he is not identical with God, and does not know all there is of God.[14]

Or it can be said that when man as a personal being knows himself as "I," he is then able to enter consciously into a relationship with infinite Personal Being who is God, who knows himself as "I am,"[15] who is within man, and who yet is also infinitely beyond man; that this is a personal relationship between self and Self, analogous to but not identical with the relationship between human self and human self; that it is profoundly affected by the relationship of the self to itself and by the relationship of the self with other human selves; that so long as man's self-knowledge is clouded by distortions of his self-understanding it is not *true* self-knowledge, hence his knowledge of God and his relationship with God will be distorted; and that in proportion as he reaches true self-understanding and true self-knowledge he is rendered the more capable of sustaining undistorted relationship with God and true firsthand knowledge of God.

This latter statement expresses briefly the position which will be developed throughout this book. But in order to keep it in balance we need to state it constantly in each of two ways: a man must know himself if he is to know God; and a man must know God if he is to know himself.

We have been saying that the self is a being. But the self is not only a being; it also is a becoming. One exists in the midst of relationships and forces to which he must make some kind of response, and in which he becomes involved as a participant. In the midst of all these, and interacting with them, he is becoming what until a given time he has not yet been, and is still further to become whatever he is yet to be. Since his *becoming* holds so large a place in all that is to follow, we shall here do no more than state the fact of becoming; and the rest of this chapter, as well as the next chapter, is devoted principally to considering various aspects of his becoming, along with some aspects of the dynamics involved in that becoming.

TOGETHERNESS AND SEPARATENESS

The human creature, in striving to become a self, requires both togetherness and separateness. His birth is a breaking of togetherness in order to gain separateness of body. But obviously he cannot maintain separate life if he does not also have togetherness with those who care for him.

From birth onward a large part of his striving goes into the effort to have both togetherness and separateness, and to hold them in such delicate balance that he will know the security of togetherness without forfeiting the security of separateness, and vice versa. If either togetherness or separateness is attained at the expense of the other, deep anxiety is aroused, for the development of selfhood is then threatened. The self instantly recognizes this situation as danger-laden and reacts against it, often at an unconscious level.

For example, if one has togetherness at the expense of separateness one feels as if he were being swallowed up, or caught in a web; thus losing or at least endangering his sense of individuality. His mental processes when awake, and dreams when asleep, will often reflect this sense of danger. It is as if he felt himself on the way to being lost in the unrelieved togetherness which claims him, threatening to imprison him or obliterate him. The prison of engulfing togetherness may be made by a parent for his child, by a child for his parent, by a brother or sister, a mate in marriage, a friend, a group of any sort, a business organization, a crowd, a mob, a mass movement, and so on almost without end.

But if one gains separateness without togetherness, communication with other selves is impaired and one begins to feel the threat of isolation. He may feel that he has to protect his separateness in order to keep from being swallowed up, and this makes communication with other selves more difficult. Or he may long to communicate deeply with other selves, but not know how. In either event the sense of isolation is likely to be reinforced, and it is somewhat as if one were trying to become a human being in a vacuum. One cannot then fully develop the attributes of a human being, or may begin to lose some of those which one already has. One is in danger of being lost in the desert of aloneness.

As we have already said, the self strives to keep the ways of meeting these two needs in balance, and to find ways to protect himself against the threat either of too great a togetherness or too great a separateness. This means, of course, that we are concerned on the one hand with the relationships of the self to other selves, and on the other hand with the relationship of the self to itself, that is, of the "I" to the "me." The first of these involves the dynamics of interpersonal relations; the second involves the dynamics of intrapsychic forces, the interplay of forces within the *psyche* or self.

These two in turn react strongly upon each other, the interpersonal dynamics upon the intrapsychic dynamics, and vice versa. The two, interpersonal and intrapsychic, cannot be separated except for purposes of thought. We do, however, so separate them for that purpose, focusing to some extent on intrapsychic dynamics throughout this chapter and the next, and focusing upon interpersonal dynamics to a certain extent throughout the rest of the book.

But this must not obscure the fact that the two are deeply intertwined. If we are asked which of the two is prior in importance, it would be almost impossible to answer. But if we are asked which is prior in time, the answer would probably have to be that the interpersonal relationships are. For in the life of an individual the dynamics of interpersonal relationships seem to govern the earliest pattern of intrapsychic dynamics in the self as infant and child.

CONCEPTS OF THE SELF

We may now turn to examine certain concepts of the self which prove to be useful. For the self is so intricate a structure of being, and so subtle in its dynamics, that we need several terms to employ as symbols for the self, whether for purposes of communication with one another, or for purposes of a deeper understanding of oneself.

The concepts about to be considered are: the potential self, the existing self, and the image of the self. The first of these is now to be taken up; the other two are considered in the following chapter.

THE POTENTIAL SELF

The human self needs to be seen both for what it is at a given point in time, which is the existing self, and for what it may become in time, which is the potential self. Without the former we soon lapse into romantic, unrealistic pictures of secular or religious Utopias dwelt in by supermen and supersaints, such as were never seen and never will be. But without keeping in view what man may become we readily sink into cynicism or despair. Of these two extremes, the first was the temptation of the latter part of the nineteenth and the early part of the twentieth century. The temptation to the second is peculiarly pressing in the middle of the twentieth century.

The potential self, of course, is the self which one may become. No one can say precisely what this is for any given person. For that reason two errors in dealing with individuals are equally possible. One is skepticism as to the potential of a particular self. This is subtly communicated as doubt of another, disbelief in his possibilities, reluctance to work with a "rotten apple," or thumbs down on him before he is given a chance to fight. Thus one self participates in establishing grounds for his doubt of another and then, seeing his doubts confirmed, takes a certain satisfaction in the soundness of his judgment.

The other error is of the opposite kind; namely, holding up expectations at so high a level that the individual can never reach them. The person thus dealt with is put on a pedestal not of his own making, and is urged to live up to his abilities, exert himself a little harder, justify the hope and toil invested in him, or keep up the family record. Under such pressures he cannot thrive, but does not know how to get down off the pedestal without severe fright to himself and severe hurt to others.

The general question of what the self may become cannot be answered except in correspondingly general terms. When we speak of certain elements in the possible self, the terms used are abstractions. In this general sense we may speak of certain capacities, remembering that the shape their development takes in actual selves is almost infinitely varied, since each self finally is unique.

Thus, in these general terms, it may be said to begin with that the individual is capable of closeness with other selves. He is capable of entering deeply and intimately into relationships which enable him both to receive and to give genuine love.

He is capable of liberation. He can withdraw from closeness when the latter threatens to engulf him. He can be freed *from* domination by other persons and by forces which are external to himself; and he can be free *to* spontaneous yet responsible living.

He is capable of community. He can enter into togetherness with a number of persons. He can participate in such group life as makes possible a measure of genuine closeness to many persons. This in turn makes possible the honest communication of feeling and thought between persons, the release of individual aptitudes into constructive activity, the planning and execution of action which expresses a common will, and all this undergirds the sense of security and worth which arises out of the experience of accepting and being accepted by one's fellows. In genuine community the self feels enhanced and stronger.

He is capable of individuality. As a self he is unique in the totality which comes into being at his birth. He is unique in the totality which he may become. His uniqueness, however, is under the constant threat of being reduced or obliterated so that he shall feel, think, and act as others do or as others try to get him to do. This is the pressure toward uniformity and conformity. But, on the negative side, he can resist these pressures. He is capable of being relatively free from striving to become what other persons try to persuade or compel him to be. He is capable also of being relatively free from striving to become some kind of self which he has idealized within himself but which in point of fact is alien to his own nature.

On the positive side of individuality, he can be relatively free to become the self which he truly is, thus fulfilling his own inward destiny. In Biblical terms the concept of individuality is implied in the term "name." The "name" denotes the unique character of an individual, the particular, intricate structure and functioning which belong to one self and to one self only in all the universe, not being duplicated in any other person now or at any other time in the entire creation.

Thus the name not only stands for the person but in a certain sense *is* the person himself. This underlies the notion, often found in magic, that to have a person's name is to have power over him. But it also underlies the profoundly spiritual idea that the name can be changed and a new name given by God.

And it underlies the immense significance attached in the Old Testament to the *name* of Jahweh, the God of Israel, and in the New Testament to the *name* of Jesus Christ the Lord. For in the ancient world there were "gods many and lords many." Visions, ecstasies, "revelations," abounded in that world. Hence distinguishing the particular identity and character, or "name," of the God of Israel and of the Lord Jesus Christ were not only essential in establishing monotheistic faith. It was essential also in defining the human self in relation to Self-revealing Deity.

Again, the self is capable of wholeness. We have already seen that the two peculiarly human capacities of self-consciousness and self-transcendence introduce into the human self the possibility of a rift. Nevertheless the human self is capable of being inwardly united into a "whole" self, thus being able to feel, think, and act as a consolidated unity.

It is difficult to describe wholeness without referring to its opposites. Thus, to be whole is *not* to be divided, split up, and the like. In logic the two terms "whole" and "individual" are closely related. For in logic "individual" means an entity which cannot be further divided; it cannot be further broken down into its component parts without destroying it. It must be taken as a whole, a unity. The analogy when we come to think of the human self is far from misleading. For the self is capable of being an undivided whole, not split up by rifts in the self. When it is not so it is in some sense a sick self.

To be whole, then, is to be *one*. To be made whole is to be integrated; hence a great deal of the modern literature on the self refers to wholeness as "integration of personality." The integrated person is one who can act as a whole, consistently and over long periods of time, with reference to self-chosen ends. He has integrity, in the sense that there is consistency between what he secretly is and what he openly is.

The state of wholeness is a state of "wholth," or health. So every discipline in which men are concerned with living organisms lays hold on this term "health" and uses it to denote a state of well-being; as in agriculture and horticulture, animal husbandry, medicine, mental hygiene, the spiritual life, to mention only a few. In all these to be in health is to be fulfilling the inward destiny which lies potentially in its root or its seed or its egg, each according to its kind. It is to be moving toward its appointed end, fulfilling its own proper function. It means showing by some appropriate outward sign that it is flourishing. And for the inward feeling of being in this good estate we have a treasury of apt expressions, such as "bursting into song."

Still again, the self is capable of creativity. He can bring into being that which was not until he took part in bringing it forth. The civilizations of the world witness to his remarkable achievements in such fields as science, architecture, painting, sculpture, music, literature, drama, technology, invention, and industry. And on a minor, but perhaps eventually no less important scale, the young and the unknown can create such works as leave no record except within themselves; yet like the great Creator they have the right to look upon what they have done and know it is good.

In some of its most important aspects creativity is a shared, not a solitary, activity. This is nowhere so impressively true as when a man and a woman together share in procreating new life in the form of a new self, a child. In this they participate in the creativity which is in God.

Once again, the self is capable of growth. There is in him a propulsive power for which there is no entirely satisfactory name. It appears to be more than the mere will to live, for that has to do first and foremost with survival. What we have in view now is more than mere survival, for it has to do with completeness. It is sometimes called "the life force" for want of a better name.

It is that which inwardly impels one, he does not know why, to pass on through various physiological and psychological stages of life until he has reached fulfillment. It is that inward cohesiveness which disposes the self to hold together and protect its own oneness under threats of disruption. It is that energizing within him which makes for health under favorable conditions or, what is more remarkable, under unfavorable ones. And it is that which makes for recovery when health has been impaired.

This life force, if we are to call it that, making for growth, health and recuperation, is one of the most remarkable powers within the human self. All who are concerned with the health and growth of persons make it their ally, rely upon it, and do homage to it, each within his own frame of reference.

These are some of the potentialities that lie within the human self. In the terminology which Christianity employs there is a concept which is of especial significance in connection with man's selfhood. It recognizes all his potentialities, recognizes his need for both togetherness and separateness, and sets all these in the context of his relation to God. This is the concept that man is created in the image of God.[16]

This concept is a symbolic representation of man's nature, and in the symbol two points of emphasis stand out. One is that man is a *creature of God*. As such he is not a small god himself, not an emanation from God, and not something which has formed itself by blind chance. Rather, he is a finite self, made by the Creator "out of the dust of the ground." He is separate from the Creator in the sense in which we have been using the word "separateness." That is, his selfhood is disengaged from that of his Maker; his selfhood is not swallowed up and obliterated in God, but he stands as it were facing God his Creator. And as a creature he shares in "creatureliness," having his place in nature as finite, and subject to all the vicissitudes of nature.

The other point of emphasis is that he is *a unique kind of creature*. All the marks of his selfhood make it possible for him not only to respond to nature, as he must; but they make it possible for him also to respond to God as he will. This can be so because the selfhood which is man is a counterpart of the Selfhood which is God, and "answers to it," at least so far as to make it possible for God to communicate with man, and for man to have the wherewithal to respond from within himself as a self-determining creature.

This means in turn that all his potentialities *can* be turned away from God and developed in conscious relation only with nature and man, which would complete his conscious and self-determined separateness from God. But it means also that all his potentialities *can* be turned toward God and developed in conscious relation with nature, man, *and God*. To do this would be to enter a deep togetherness with God as self with Self, and thus to fulfill his own selfhood without in any sense undermining that selfhood or forsaking his integrity. It would signify that a man is responding with his deepest "Yes" in a relationship with the Other who is within him and yet beyond him, a relationship wherein he can fully find himself and truly know himself.

But there are threats to human selfhood which are still to be considered, in view of which all of man's relationships, actual and potential, take on an even greater depth of meaning. To these we now turn.

CHAPTER II

Threats to the Self

A SECOND CONCEPT of the self to be examined is that of the existing
self.

THE EXISTING SELF

Whereas "the potential self" refers to what the self may become, "the existing self" refers to the self as it exists in a particular
moment in time. Discussion of the potential self tends almost un-
avoidably to suggest the posed picture, where everything is in
place and the smile is exactly right. Discussion of the existing self
is needed as a corrective, for this yields a picture more like a
"candid camera shot" of a man caught off guard in the rush of
things as they are.

The concept of the existing self connotes the fact that when
the self is enmeshed in actual living and forgets to try to feel nice,
act nice, and look nice, he is an intricate mingling of opposites and
contradictions. Consider, for example, how common it is for such
opposites as these to exist within one and the same self: love and
hate, kindness and cruelty, considerateness and ruthlessness, courage and fear, satisfaction and discontent, conscious and unconscious
motives tangled together and competing with each other; great-
ness and meanness, hope and despair.

As with the potential self, so with the existing self: each self
is highly particularistic. There is no other like it. In the true sense
it is unique. It has a highly personal history, much of it being of an
intensely intimate kind. The personal history of any one person
is seldom if ever fully known by any other human being.

This shape of things as they have been and now are is peculiar to the one self as to lead him to feel that no one else *fully* understands him. And when anxiety mounts in him he feels that he does not understand himself. This double feeling of not being understood and not understanding oneself grows the more disturbing in proportion as togetherness is lost and as community grows stereotyped and artificial or breaks down, for then the self is the more walled in, in his separateness. This is one of the reasons why so many persons now are willing to pay large sums to one other person with whom they may try to communicate in depth for many hours in full security, regarding the actual situation in the self's own inner world.

Here we can do no more than deal with a few abstractions drawn out from the situations of many existing selves. The statements about to follow are in no sense proposed as pictures of existing individuals, but only as postures of the self which many persons have in common.

First to be observed is the fact that the existing self carries a deep anxiety, either potential or active. This anxiety is an intense but vague apprehensiveness. It is a foreboding of danger or even of disaster, and yet one cannot put his finger on the danger which threatens him. One feels acutely that he is in some kind of peril, yet the feeling is so diffuse that he cannot tell *what* the peril is. It appears, moreover, that anxiety begins at the moment of birth. Only much later, if one survives, can he begin the attempt to give a rational, verbal account of the "reasons" for his anxiety.

The subject of anxiety has received so much attention in recent times as to lead many to ask whether anxiety is as deep and as widespread as is often asserted; or whether on the contrary it is nearer the truth to say that anxiety is being aggravated by so much discussion of it. There is no doubt that anxiety can be stirred up by talking about it. This may take any one of many forms, such as being anxious to feel anxious if other people do, or of feeling anxious when others say that anxiety is common and we wish for some reason to deny it.

But when all of this is admitted, a far more important situation has to be faced. This is the inward situation which exists in many persons down at a level where casual discussion and logical argument have little effect. That this inward situation is widespread, among people of all ages and conditions of life, there can be no doubt. For those who communicate with other selves at a deep level know of anxiety so profound in any one person, and common to so many persons, as to constitute a phenomenon of present existence which cannot be ignored.

Rollo May in his study of anxiety, after reviewing an extensive literature on the subject, observes that anxiety derives its powerfully disturbing quality from the fact that selfhood itself is under threat. As May puts it, "the security base itself of the individual is threatened and since it is in terms of this security base that the individual has been able to experience himself as a self in relation to objects, the distinction between subject and object also breaks down."[1]

In a state of anxiety, as said, there is a deep, but vague and painful, apprehensiveness. But the subject, the self-conscious "I," cannot locate the "cause," or perhaps moves about from one "reason" to another, trying to account for the diffused unease within him. He cannot succeed in objectifying the anxiety, or if he seems to succeed temporarily he soon has to repeat the effort. He cannot succeed in objectifying the anxiety because the anxiety registers a state of peril within the person himself, as a self. With intuitive wisdom which is deeper than any rational processes, the self senses this as deadly peril. And indeed it is literally that. *For it is the existence of the self as a self which is in danger. The consciousness of being a self is under threat and is being undermined.*

Hence it is the self itself which needs to be established or re-established, and enhanced. But to recognize this situation in any profound sense is itself painful in the extreme in that it is felt as an admission of helplessness, a surrender to the encroaching dissolution and eventual extinction of the self.

Since anxiety registers so profound, but also so vague, a danger, it is readily converted into symptoms or into fears. Symptoms provide something concrete to be cared for. Fears provide something specific to flee from or to attack. Both symptoms and fears provide something specific outside the citadel of the self, the "I,"

One may, however, be the object of too great a closeness. This kind of closeness often assumes the disguise of "love," but holds one in a bondage where genuine love is impossible. In such instances it is common to find that hostility flourishes, too great to be concealed and yet too frightening to be expressed except in indirect ways.

Again, the existing self may not be able to attain liberation. For whatever reason, he finds himself dominated. The domination may be exerted by other persons, or by institutions, or by vast impersonal forces outside himself, against which he feels himself powerless. He feels himself being manipulated and resents it, resents the persons or forces that manipulate him, and resents himself for allowing himself to be manipulated; and yet can find no way to break out from under the domination.

He then may find that he must hide the resentment and "play the game" for stakes which, if he wins them, only bind him more securely in the bondage which he inwardly loathes. And to compound the threat, superficial efforts to find a way to live under such conditions are likely to be lauded as "wonderful resignation," "making a good adjustment," and so on. John P. Marquand's novel *Point of No Return* is a story of the way this vicious circle operates. A young couple strive for advancement in a banking house only to realize that with each step upward in the organization they have tied themselves more firmly in the web of frustration; and yet they cannot go back, for that would be "failure."

Yet again the self, though capable of community, may fail to find it; or, finding it, may be inwardly unable to enter deeply into it. The mobile nature of modern populations makes the quest for community doubly difficult for many. For in addition to whatever degree of drawing back from community they may carry within themselves, they must move about so much as to make it very difficult for them to let their roots go down. The displaced persons of modern times are not only those who have been uprooted by the direct impact of war and defeat. They are also, often, uprooted by participation in victory, in success, and in the great impersonal process called production.

Such persons as are unable to enter deeply into community

live in some degree of isolation. In the case of relative but not complete isolation, one may maintain enough communication to enable him to live as a partially social being, in the midst of community but not participating richly in it. In this case one will probably be called an individualist, and will perhaps be praised for his independence. Or he may be called "a lone wolf," "a bit peculiar," and be left the more to himself.

In the case of virtually complete isolation, one may become "antisocial" in such forms as the person who "is a law unto himself," the recluse, the delinquent, the criminal. But on the other hand he may retire more and more completely into himself until he "loses contact" and is known as mentally ill.

In becoming isolated one is not merely being alienated from community. In becoming alienated from community one is also being alienated from himself. As we have seen, he requires separateness in order to become a self, but even before that he requires togetherness. And as separateness becomes isolation the boundaries between the self as it is and the world as it is begin to grow indistinct. The self begins to create an unreal world of its own to live in, peopled by unreal persons to live with in fantasy. In thus overcoming the limitations of reality he overrides the boundaries of his own selfhood and begins to obliterate them from within. True selfhood is being impaired or lost.

This is one reason why in therapy the boundaries of the self have to be reestablished from within by making genuine choices, "acts of will," in the face of real alternatives, and without external pressure. Doing this in a relationship with another self is reentering community. If true and deep community had been possible earlier, the boundaries of the self would probably not have been endangered or lost as the self tried to develop.

Further, the existing self may fall short of what can properly be called individuality.[4] Striving for it, he may succeed only in becoming "odd." But perhaps it is more likely that, not having achieved firm ground for the consciousness of being a self, he will lack the foundation for self-respect. He may feel himself "a nobody," a mere cog in a machine, a serial number but not a name, a bit of flotsam, a "hand" to toil for others while not knowing what he wants to do for himself.

This feeling of threatened or lost identity haunts many in schools, in cities, in factories, in great business organizations, in the armed forces, in devastated lands. It is a homesickness for selfhood on the part of those who have begun to be a self, but are not firmly consolidated in selfhood, and must live in contact with others who treat them as things. Thus a girl of seven, who had come to a great city to live, was asked, "How do you like the people here?" She replied, "Well, they are all right—they talk to you but their voice doesn't pay you any attention."

It would seem that the feeling of lost identity and hence of threatened selfhood can be borne only so long, and then, as we say, "something has to give way." Leon J. Saul, who served as a psychiatrist in the Second World War, believes that each person has his "point of vulnerability"; when that is reached he can tolerate no more. Naturally this point will vary from one person to another. But the question of where the breaking point lay was not merely a question of how much physical danger and discomfort a man could endure. Frequently the invasion of a man's selfhood by military authority could be borne only up to a point. For example, one man, who was not greatly troubled by danger and hardship, "exploded" when ordered to have his hair cut in a certain prescribed way. That was one thing too many.[5]

Then there is the condition wherein the self, although capable of wholeness, exists in some kind of splitness. Such splitness is always finally highly peculiar to the one self who suffers it. It thus is a highly particularistic condition, arising out of the individual's own personal history, and hence needing to be understood on its own ground as intensely personal. Nevertheless, as Arnold Toynbee has shown, there may be forms of "schism in the soul" which become so common at a given period as to characterize a group or even a civilization.[6]

Splitness in the self may take any of many possible forms, in the individual. For example, it may consist of trying to carry out incompatible purposes; or being unable to achieve any purpose at all, as when it looks as if a person is always standing in the way of his own success, no matter what he tries; or pursuing one purpose with zest for a little while only to drop it and take up another. Or it may express itself in fluctuating, unstable moods.

Splitness in the self may show up as some form of pronounced onesidedness. Thus it may appear in the attempt to cultivate the mind while neglecting the body, or vice versa. It may appear as homage to the intellect and its works, accompanied by contempt of feeling; or vice versa.

Splitness in the self very often makes its appearance under the name of conscience and high ideals. Thus under the guise of conscience one may exhaust himself in trying to throttle his natural impulses without being able to incorporate them into his total scheme of life, striving always to keep them pushed back into the far hinterland of the self and yet unable to forget them. Or splitness may take the form of "holding" tenaciously to very high ideals, admittedly out of all possible reach, but not to be surrendered since to do that would be to commit treason against himself, he supposes. In this uncomfortable position he can cling to his ideals, and judge others by them, thus reaching an uneasy peace with himself.

Splitness takes on a certain halo when the self, dissatisfied with itself, goes into the business of self-improvement. The "I" then starts to work on the "me" to make it better, more presentable to oneself and others, pruning off something here, grafting in something there, rather pleased with itself for its earnestness.

Taking a different road to splitness, one may devote himself to the fullest possible satisfaction of natural impulses. There must be no inhibitions. The bars are down. This kind of splitness, however, is enjoyed at the cost of a withering capacity for moral judgment upon one's own manner of life.

It will be evident that many kinds of splitness have their roots in man's capacity for self-transcendence. Many forms of splitness arise because the self is condemning and rejecting itself on grounds of some kind of felt unworthiness. Psychoanalysis has made us aware of the depth of this problem. But it no longer seems possible to say, as once was claimed, that religious teaching produces the problem of man's self-rejection and self-condemnation, although of course a strongly moralistic religious teaching may aggravate it. It now seems far nearer the truth to say that religion is among other things a way of undertaking to solve a profound problem in the achieving of selfhood, a problem which man himself produces spontaneously from within himself.

And we are now able freshly to understand that spiritual religion has a profound solution for the problem. But we can also better understand afresh that religion as practiced and offered often touches only the surface, not the depth, of man's alienation from himself. For in the very household of religion, that is, in the Christian community, are many persons who continue in self-condemnation and are unable to accept reconciliation either with themselves, with other persons, or with God.

All these kinds of splitness represent civil war within the self. Commonly they are accompanied by self-hate, often at an unconscious level, and by some form of self-punishment. The prevalence of psychosomatic disorders in persons of every age seems to testify to the damage wrought by this civil war within the self; to say nothing of other forms of self-crippling disturbance, each with its own kind of damage. For so long as there is a middle wall of partition within the self to keep the self from being reconciled with itself, all other reconciliations are blocked.

As for creativity, it is not difficult to see that any of the conditions we have been describing might undermine creativity. The energies of the self, being expended in the effort to protect the self, tend to be drawn off in such directions as getting away from the danger, or fighting it. Thus, and especially in the latter case, destructivity replaces creativity. Hatred and fear are called out, rather than love and confidence. Persuading himself that his hatred is righteous anger, one may release immense energy in the effort to destroy a reputation, a rival, a competitor, an institution, a state, a culture. Here emerges the constantly recurring Samson motif: the will to destroy oneself in order to destroy the foe and wreck what he has built up.

War, of course, is the classic example of destructivity expressed under social sanction. War has many forms, not all of them employing physical weapons. Men, their work and their reputations, are destroyed by special techniques of cooperative action under the name of business or a profession or a trade or loyalty to Americanism or to religion.

But it must not be forgotten that the opposite may happen; namely, that creativity of a high order may be called forth by the very dangers which threaten the self. This can take place, for example, as a result of normal anxiety. In normal anxiety, as we have seen, the very foundation of selfhood is threatened. But by exercising creativity the foundation of selfhood is affirmed and strengthened, and the self is more firmly established in the face of the threats to its existence.

Once more, there is the question of what happens to the self's capacity for growth. The existing self, falling short of its potential, is to that extent falling short of its possibilities of growth. Growth may, for example, be retarded, or arrested; or one may regress to some earlier stage from which he cannot again emerge.

Many recent workers have examined the status of the existing self from the standpoint of one's maturing. These studies are especially valuable in showing a sort of cross section of the existing self at a given time in life when growth has gone forward adequately, or when on the other hand it has been distorted.[7]

THE IMAGE OF THE SELF

We have seen that we need to take into account the potential self and the existing self. We have now to take into account also the image of himself which one has when he thinks of himself. We have already seen that in self-transcendence the self is capable, so to speak, of standing outside itself and watching itself. The question now is, "What does the self 'see' when it thinks of itself?"

In taking up such a question it is well to distinguish three kinds of ideas of himself which one may have in thinking of himself. One of these is the concept, which is a *general* idea. That is to say, one may think of himself as being something which one shares in common with many other selves, such as a privileged person or an oppressed one; or he may think of himself as a white man, black man, and so on in relation to race or color.

He thus knows himself as one of a general class of persons. The fact that he finds himself in a class, and indeed in many classes at once, is a source of dynamic within the self. He may, for example, resent his class status; or he may try to ignore it and protest even the use of the word "class"; or he may have a keen class consciousness, trying to guard the interests of his class, arguing for its importance.

In any case his general idea of himself gives him that much ground for a sense of community with many other persons with whom he has at least this much in common. The general idea of class or classes, embodied in the image of the self, is capable of strongly fortifying the feeling of togetherness. But it begins to become a hazard to the broader sense of community as soon as walls are run up around those who have most in common.

Again, one may come to have an *abstract* idea of himself. That is, he may be able in thought to lift out qualities or capacities which he shares in common with a very great number of men, or with all men. Thus he may say, "I am a human being," or "I am anxious because I am finite as all men are," and the like.

Although these are abstract ideas, it would be a grave misunderstanding to regard abstract ideas of the self as lacking in dynamic quality. Quite the contrary is true. The taking in of abstract ideas of the human being and clothing these with passion is one of the dynamic forces in history. Dealing with the great abstractions concerning man and his relation with his fellows and with God is one of the major functions of the Christian community. For the great abstractions represent man's attempt not only to grasp the meaning of his own existence, but to grasp also the meaning of that which he shares in common with all men. They are among the imperatives if there is to be an ever widening community.

There is also the *specific* idea which one has when he thinks of himself, not as being in this or that classification, and not as possessing this or that abstract quality, but as an individual person. This highly specific idea may be called his image of himself. To be sure, it may contain elements drawn from his store of general and abstract ideas. But now all is fused into the image of one person: "Myself." The image of the self, we may say then, is what the "I" perceives when it looks at the "me." Perhaps it is no accident that in common English usage we want to say, "This is me," grammar to the contrary notwithstanding.

The image of the self is so deeply tinged by the physical factors of existence that some prefer to call it outright "the body image." This is done at the risk of underrating the importance of intrapsychic forces which have little to do with the body as such. Nevertheless it serves as a reminder that the size, shape, appearance, and functioning of one's body are associated with many of the most intensely personal and highly concrete experiences of his existence. Memories of these body experiences contain the most minute detail. And anticipation of future experiences often turns on some question as to how the body or some part of it will behave, or how others will respond to it.

Moreover, the body image in many instances is intensely painful to the one who thinks "This is me." This is true not only of those who regard their bodies as ugly, unattractive, or inadequate. Great beauty is sometimes painful also, since one may feel that he or she attracts others by the surface, not by the depth, of the self.

The fact that the body image is so painful, and so hard to speak of, often causes one to conceal both the image and the distress it causes, with the result that his anxiety seeks a disguised and more approved form of expression. This in turn may induce one to present psychological or religious "problems" which are actually of secondary importance to him as a self, but which are acceptable "problems" for one to have in his milieu. This is one of many reasons why the opening questions in a discussion of religious matters are often so unimportant.

But even when the importance of the body image is fully admitted, the broader term "the image of the self" is to be preferred if it is kept in mind that the body image is contained within the larger concept of the image of the self. Thus the fact is kept in view that the self is functioning through a specific body, and that one's image of himself is probably not long wanting in the particular details of his own body.

In considering the image of the self, there is one question which is basic. Does one's image of himself correspond faithfully to what one really is, or is there a discrepancy between what one is and what one thinks he is? If the image of the self corresponds faithfully and fully to what one is, it is to be supposed that the individual then has complete self-understanding and self-knowledge. He will not only know truth about himself. He will *be* truth embodied in living form.

But commonly, and perhaps always, there is some discrepancy between what the self is, and what he sees himself as being. In that case the image of the self does not correspond fully and faithfully to reality. There is then some form or some degree of untruth within the self in its relation to itself.

The discrepancy between the reality and the image of the self varies greatly from one person to another, ranging from the very slight and not very serious, to the extreme discrepancy which is found, for example, in paranoid systems of thought when one holds delusions of persecution or of grandeur. It would seem that the discrepancy itself begins to arise when one's image of himself commences to be distorted by pressures which the self feels but is not able to handle. In other words, prolonged anxiety may distort the image of the self.

There is one kind of distorted image of the self which has received especial attention in recent years; namely, the idealized image of the self. Karen Horney, who seems to have introduced the term, meant by it the image of themselves which some neurotic persons have. As she defined it, the idealized image is "an image of what the neurotic believes himself to be, or of what at that time he feels he can or ought to be."[9] And she has showed how the individual, with his idealized image of himself as a sort of base, can build up a "pride system" and assert his "neurotic claims" upon himself and others.[10]

Several features of the idealized image stand out as especially significant in such considerations as we are here examining. One is the fact that the idealized image is unreal; that is, it does not correspond with what a given self really is. This means that the self's relation to itself is constructed on a foundation of falsity. But there is the further fact that this kind of falsity in the self is, or at least underlies and accompanies, a sickness in the self. This kind of sickness is now commonly called "neurotic."

A third feature of the situation is the fact that the kind of sickness which results from or accompanies the idealized image impairs the self in the very effort one is making to find himself. For it impairs one's consciousness of being a self, it impairs one's understanding of his own potentiality, and it undermines his ability to take responsibility as a mature person.

Perhaps the most searching consideration for all who have a concern over what happens to persons in the Christian community is the fact that pressures emanating from a misunderstanding of religion may serve to strengthen or even help to create an idealized image of the self. In this event religion, instead of leading to "truth in the inward parts," leads to fortifying a falsity within the self.

One of the principal ways by which an idealized image of the self is built up is heavy emphasis upon what one ought to do. Under subtle but powerful pressures the individual may construct his detailed image of what *he* ought to do. Then any one of many possible results may begin to follow. We may take two typical results as examples.

A person may come to believe that in fact he is doing just what he ought to do, and be proud of it. He sees himself, perhaps, as something of a saint, and begins to play that role. This is the man whom the Bible refers to as the hypocrite, that is, the person who is acting out the role of the "very good" man on the stage of life, and is carefully watching every act so that it will be morally correct. The standard of what is morally correct is carefully worked out, and observed to the letter. But being a performer of a role, he cannot act out of integrity and spontaneity. So this is not living from deep within the self; it is "playing up" to his idealized image of the good man.

Another typical result is somewhat the opposite. One knows that he is not doing what he ought to do; the harder he tries, the more he fails, until perhaps he is overwhelmed by the sense of his own shortcoming and transgression, and yet knows no way to forsake his moralism without incurring still greater peril. He is imprisoned by the demands which his idealized image lays upon him, but to break out would mean branding himself as a lost soul.

A young man who understands how the idealized image can make one a captive to himself by means of moralism writes thus of the interior situation which resulted in his own life:

The Prisoner. He walked alone down the narrow path that angled over the wasteland. There was no place else to walk but in the hard, uncompromising narrowness that was the path. All else was a threatening yellow wasteland; the sun beat down upon an abysmal lifeless wilderness. . . . To step off the well-defined limits of the path with its angular sharpness was to feel the terrible anxiety of the unknown. . . . But the wasteland was an illusion of his own making. There was no life there because it was he who could not see life. He could not see life because he did not have life . . . a dying man called the world dead and himself alive. Yet part of him knew it was an illusion.[11]

Taking it all in all, then, the image of the self is deeply involved in the intrapsychic dynamics of the self. And religion, philosophy, psychiatry, and psychotherapy have this in common: they represent a concern that the self should so think of itself as to root this intrapsychic dynamic in truth, not in falsity, as this image is shaped and reshaped within the self.[12]

THE PREDICAMENT OF NORMAL ANXIETY

We should now recapitulate, in order to bring matters into focus before we begin to ask whether the Christian community and Christian faith are relevant to the deeper aspects of the situation of the human self.

We have seen that there are certain essential marks of being a human self. The self has vitality; it is a living body which is a totality. It exercises self-determination, which means that it can choose, can will its own acts, can set and reset its own limits of action, and can initiate action from within the self. It has *self*-consciousness, which is the consciousness that one *is* a self, an "I," a particular identity which can know itself as a self.

It is self-transcendent; which means among other things that man is both a moral and a spiritual being. He is moral, because he sits in judgment upon himself to accuse or else to excuse himself. He is spiritual because, although a member of the animal kingdom, he often moves about in a kingdom which "is not of this world" in the sense that he is moved by intangibles, and seeks to orient himself to the whole of reality beyond the limits of time and space. And from that vantage point which is within him and yet also beyond him, he passes judgment upon his judgment of himself.

Thus even if he should say, "I am no more than animal," he has transcended himself in order to reach that judgment upon himself and his doings. He has betrayed his hunger to know what he is in the total scheme of things, or a hunger to know whether there is even "a scheme of things" at all. He has exercised his humanity even if only in order to deny it.

We have seen that the self has potentialities which probably are never fully realized. In particular we spoke of man's capacity for closeness, for liberation, for community, for individuality, for wholeness, for creativity, and for growth.

But we have seen also that under the conditions of human existence as we know it *every point in the foundations of selfhood is under threat.* This holds true with regard to vitality, or life in a body; with regard to self-determination, self-consciousness, and self-transcendence; and with regard to every potentiality which he carries within himself.

Here is perhaps the greatest mystery of all being and becoming: not merely that being *is* and becoming *is possible,* although this mystery itself is utterly beyond our comprehension; but the still greater mystery that the same universe which offers these possibilities seems also at the same time to oppose them. *And we do not even know how to state truly and fully the nature of this mystery. But under the conditions of human existence we experience this mystery as anxiety.*

We may call this situation *the predicament of normal anxiety.* It is predicament in many senses. It has befallen us to live in a world which arouses anxiety. We did not make it so, although of course we may aggravate it. But that is the way it is. It confronts us. We cannot wish it away by forgetting it, or by denying it, or by throwing the bright light of optimism upon it.

It is profound: it does its work down at the foundations. It arises out of, and at the same time threatens, the very bases upon which human selfhood can be formed.

It yields to no easy solution. This is true partly because anxiety itself is diffuse, and quickly seizes upon some enemy or problem to attack, only to discover that this is not the real foe nor the real issue. And it is true partly because the anxiety which creates the need for a rational solution invades the very processes of rational thinking by means of which we hope to reach a solution.

And any solution which we can find for the predicament of normal anxiety leads sooner or later to a new predicament. Thus if we seek to live entirely without anxiety we incur the risk of forfeiting the very marks of our humanity itself, since it is just these which make us capable of anxiety. And yet we cannot live in an unrelieved state of even normal anxiety without risking the deterioration or the extinction of self-transcendence, self-consciousness, self-determination, and eventually vitality itself.

This predicament of normal anxiety is a timeless one, not peculiar to any one people or any one place. The myths of mankind bear abundant testimony to the recognition of anxiety as the common lot of men. Take but a single example. At Chichén Itzá in Yucatan, in the midst of the ruins of the ancient Mayan civilization, many pieces of bas-relief sculpture have survived. One of these plaques seems to mean that tears are the ground out of which all forms of life spring and are nourished. But in this plaque it is not only shown that tears are the ground of life. The tears themselves are the tears of a god.

*　　*　　*

In Christianity there is a remarkable combination of two opposites held in creative tension with each other. It is a religion of tragedy, in that it seeks not to hide its face from any aspect of man's predicament. But it is a religion of hope and joy, in that it understands how tragedy can be transcended. It is a religion of the Cross, yet it is a singing religion, in which the dirge gives way to the songs of triumph.

We turn now to inquire why this is so; and how the power to become triumphant is communicated.

CHAPTER III

The Christian Community

In what has preceded, attention has been given largely to the individual aspects of existence. Now it needs to be turned toward the community aspects of existence, where persons live in some kind of relationship with one another.

RELATIONSHIPS IN COMMUNITY

The term "community" implies that persons sustain some kind of relationship with one another. When persons are brought into association with one another, relationships are set up between them. The relationships may be felt as closeness, or as distance. In any case when persons are brought to bear upon one another relationships of some kind start up between them.

A "relationship" in its simplest form is that which exists *between* two entities and affects them both, when they are brought to bear upon each other. This "betweenness" is a dynamic field in which each entity "does something to" the other, such as attracting, staying neutral, or repelling.

If this is put in terms of human relationships, when two persons are brought to bear upon each other they "do something to" each other, whether it is building each other up, or tearing each other down, or whatever else. *What* they do to each other is a function of the relationship that exists between them; that is, it depends upon the nature of the relationship between them. The *process* of affecting each other in relationships is *interaction between persons.*

If we take more complex cases where several persons are in

interaction, the same principles hold. For relationships may exist among several persons, as in a family or in any other group. Here also persons are interacting in relationships and in doing so are affecting one another. This too is a dynamic field, but an extremely complicated one. It is an intricate network of crisscrossing relationships, such as the relationship of each person to every other person, person to person through a third person, person to group, and group to person.

Moreover the field of interrelatedness and interaction is highly sensitive, being subject to sudden shifts of feeling. For example, a group may at one time engage itself in building up one of its members, but at another time may turn upon him and begin savagely to "take him to pieces." But here, as in the simpler case of the one-to-one relationship, *what* happens within the persons involved depends upon the nature of the relationships between them; the *process* of its happening is interaction between persons.

Relationships and interaction are of the highest importance for two reasons among many. The first of these is that they appear to determine the character structure of the individual self. We have in view here a generalization which seems to be justified by the findings in many branches of psychological study, and which seems also to be borne out by studies of the past. It is this. *The self is formed in its relationships with others. If it becomes de-formed, it becomes so in its relationships. If it is re-formed or trans-formed, that too will be in its relationships.*

The expression "in a relationship" as here used means not only within it, but in virtue of the interaction between selves which takes place. In any such statement we must allow, of course, for congenital deficiencies of mind or body, and for inroads upon the body by diseases which impair the physical organism. But we are thinking now of the self which one *becomes*, whatever his endowment. This becoming, it appears, is a becoming in and by virtue of relationships, according as one's native endowment and native potentialities will allow.

The other reason for the high importance of relationships and interaction is the reverse of what has just been said. It may be expressed in this summary but simple way: *a community is a body of*

relationships which affect the becoming of its individual members.
A community "does something to" the people who compose it, and
they in turn do something to *it,* as the people of the community interact with one another.

The relationships which carry the greatest power to affect the
character structure of the young self are those that exist within that
most intimate of all forms of community, the family. In our culture
ordinarily the earliest years are spent in the midst of whatever relationships the young self sustains with the mother or the mother
substitute, the father or the father substitute, the siblings, if any,
and whoever else makes up the household. In the case of those who
do not grow up in a household, the same point still holds; namely,
that one grows up in the midst of a body of relationships.

It appears further that in those early years the character structure begins to take shape long before the child is able to talk. Indeed, there is much evidence to support the view that the character
structure begins to take its form from the day of birth, of course
within the limits of one's native endowment and potentialities.[1]

The relationships in which the young grow up *seem always in
actual life to contain some kind of mingling of creative and destructive interaction.* Of course, these relationships may be, and very
often are, of the highest possible order. In that event they tend to
affirm the selfhood of the young, and to lead toward the realization of the potential self. But they may, and it would seem that they
commonly do, also contain some element of greater or lesser
strength which threatens the full realization of the potential self.
With this basic character structure, whether for better or for
worse, the very young begin to move out little by little from the
circle of the family.

As the younger person begins to move out from the smaller
orbit of the family into a larger orbit, he is seeking some kind of
relationship and some kind of interaction which the members of
his family cannot supply. In doing so he encounters others who are
in a generally similar situation. These all are seeking community,
whether in play groups or clique or club or gang. The resulting
tightly knit togetherness of the young with their own kind in
some form of community is a notable feature of the transition from

the relatively safe community of the family to the psychologically hazardous situation of those who are just coming into physical maturity.

In maturity the search for community commonly continues, as people seek to associate themselves with others in some form of togetherness. Nor does the search for community cease with the passing of the decades. To the end of life there is the need to be bound up together in some manner with others of our kind. This is the more important as aging comes, whether for those who have known profoundly satisfying family life, only to find it breaking up around them; or for those who have not known it and now feel that the coming of the last years carries the threat of devastating loneliness at the end.

The need for community is no respecter of social and economic levels. But finding it is another matter. The poor, needing community, often can find it only in the fact of their poverty. The desperate need it, but often can find common ground only in the feeling that every man's hand is against them. The comfortably well off perhaps find it easier than any others to attain community with their kind. The very wealthy and their children perhaps find it harder than any others to attain deep community, being shut out from so much of the common lot of men, and exposed to so many persons who cultivate acquaintance with some concealed motive.

All these, the young, the desperate, the poor, and the wealthy, different though they are in so many other ways, have this in common: they live under the threat of being excluded from the deepest community so that they are pushed into partial community or into separateness. They share also a healthy suspicion of being "taken in" by any kind of community which will try to exploit them.

Hence the deeper need for community is a need for a kind of community in which the bond of association is some concern which is held in common. No concern they share in common is any more profound than the desire to find oneself and be a person in one's own right, regardless of age or status, regardless of poverty or wealth.

Beyond all this it is being borne home to us now that the right to be man which the small communities of men attempt to guarantee to their members is under threat from the schism between sovereign national states, and especially from the great schism between the West and the East. These forms of schism make up the great splitness in the world as a whole which now holds the fear of destruction before all men's eyes.

In the face of this threat there seems to be a great ground swell of longing for "one world" in which not only nations but individual men live under law to which all are subject, not under fear. To attain this is a political task. But how is this to be attained apart from a reconciliation between men so deeply rooted in the spirits of men that the common will to peace will brook no more delay? This is a spiritual task.

Community, then, as we are considering it here, has a threefold aspect. People seek community with others not only for the sake of togetherness as such, but for the sake also of supplying deficiencies in the relationships they have already known. In such community as they find, they affect and are affected by others in interaction with them. And the interaction commonly contains the two elements so often called to attention; namely, both potentially constructive, and potentially destructive, forces.

Thus the community which one finds may, on the one hand, provide the opportunity for creative interaction in relationships which may reduce or even remove some of the threats which one feels, so enhancing selfhood. In this way some of the deficiencies in the existing self may be supplied, or an already healthy character structure may be further supported and strengthened. But on the other hand the community which one finds may involve him in the kind of interaction which reinforces the threats that he already feels, or may even produce new ones to which he has been a stranger until now. In this event the community which he finds tends to undermine a character structure which was already weak, and may begin to tear down one which was healthy.

Persons, of course, seek many kinds of community. Perhaps no one kind of community can supply all the legitimate needs for community which any one person feels. It is not our purpose to consider, or even attempt to name, them all. Instead, we turn now more specifically to the *Christian* community.

THE NATURE OF THE CHRISTIAN COMMUNITY

When we ask about the nature of the Christian community we must, of course, ask about the nature of the Christian church. The term "the Christian community" is but one name among many for the Christian church, bringing out one of its aspects. But the moment we begin to inquire into the nature of the church we are met by a surprising fact which George Florovsky, among many, has called to attention. He writes: "It is impossible to start with a formal definition of the church. For strictly speaking there is none which can claim any doctrinal authority."[2]

He goes on to say that no definition is to be found in the Fathers, nor in the schoolmen, not even in St. Thomas Aquinas. None was given by the Ecumenical Councils, and none by the Great Councils, including those of Trent and the Vatican. He continues, quoting from Bartmann, "The church existed for about fifteen hundred years without reflecting upon its nature and without attempting its clarification by a logical conception."[3] And he adds:

In our time, it seems, one has to get beyond the modern theological disputes to regain a wider historical perspective, to recover the true "catholic mind," which would embrace the whole of the historical experience of the church in its pilgrimage through the ages. One has to return from the schoolroom to the worshiping church and perhaps to change the school-dialect of theology for the pictorial and metaphorical language of Scripture. The very nature of the church can be rather depicted and described than properly defined. And surely this can be done only from within the church. Probably even this description will be convincing only for those of the church. The Mystery is apprehended only by faith.[4]

We have referred to Florovsky's statement at this length for two reasons. The first is that the church's experience through a span of many centuries is comparable with that of a healthy-minded individual, in that it had the strong self-consciousness of being a church; and as long as it was sure of itself it experienced itself as a unique entity without needing to stop and consciously define itself. The second reason is that the church, again like the individual, has to be experienced from within in order to be known. And as Florovsky suggests, this knowing of itself from within consists primarily in *knowing itself as a worshiping community*.

Our task, then, is to try to identify and briefly state some of the principal ways in which a Christian community experiences itself and knows itself as a worshiping community.

In the first place, the Christian community is a self-transcending community and knows itself as such, however the matter may be expressed from one communion to another. In saying this we are not forgetting the fact that a particular Christian community, a "local church," is embedded in the social order. It is set down in a particular locality. It owns property. It is subject to, and is protected by, civil law. It has some kind of stake, large or small, in the *status quo*. It is sensitive to cultural conditions, for its people are people of a particular time and place. A great deal more could be said in recognition of the church's inextricable involvement in the world as it is.

Nevertheless as a Christian community it transcends all this even while remaining in it. For so soon as it begins to act corporately it orients itself to another dimension and knows itself to be rooted and grounded in that other dimension. The nature of that other dimension is indicated at once, for example, by the very word for community which it uses. That word is *koinonia*, which means fellowship, communion, sharing, participating in, the state of being in communication; in short, *koinonia is* community.

But *koinonia* is a kind of community which transcends ordinary human community in that God is present and participant in the community. For the connotation of *koinonia* is that *the Spirit of God is forthgoing into, and present in, every relationship within the community*. Thus it signifies that every relationship in the Christian community participates in God and God in it, whether it be the relationship of person to person, or of each to all, or all to each; while the whole community as a whole participates in God and God in it. Thus *koinonia* is by its nature a community intimately indwelt by the Spirit.

The orientation of the Christian community to God from whom it has its being is of course symbolized in many ways. For example, the Long Meter Doxology, used in many congregations at the opening of the service of worship, voices it in the familiar words:

> Praise God, from whom all blessings flow;
> Praise him, all creatures here below;
> Praise him above, ye heavenly host;
> Praise Father, Son, and Holy Ghost.

And the equally familiar Apostolic Benediction with which the assemblage is often dismissed, contains the word *koinonia:* "The grace of the Lord Jesus Christ, and the love of God, and the communion of the Holy Spirit be with you all"; which is saying, at the very end of the moments spent together in worship, "Let this communion go out with you unbroken into whatever is before you."

The idea of a community which transcends itself is wrapped up in many of the familiar words for the church. Indeed, the word "church" itself does this; for an *ecclesia,* or church, is an assemblage of those who have been "called out," and "the church of God" is those who have been called out from the world by God, to meet God. Again, it is "the Body of Christ," to denote a prolonging of that Self in bodily form to the end of time.

In Scripture it is called by many names which indicate its self-transcendent nature. It is "the house of God," "the household of God," "the household of faith," where the idea of the church as a family, men as brothers, and God as Father, is prominent. There are terms which express the idea of a living organism, like a body or a plant, having Jesus Christ as the head of the body or the trunk of the plant. There are terms that express the idea of the believer's body as a temple of the Spirit, and the community as a living temple built out of living stones; and numerous others. In all of them the suggestion of the community's organic togetherness with that togetherness indwelt by God is strong.

The self-transcendence of the Christian community is affirmed in the act of worship itself. In worship men turn beyond themselves and affirm God. This is true, for example, in prayer in such acts as adoration, thanksgiving, confession, supplication for one-self, and intercession for others.

Self-transcendence is affirmed by the sacraments. There we are confronted by the body and blood of Jesus Christ during the sacrament of holy communion, and we are confronted by the Spirit of God during the sacrament of baptism. Similarly during such other sacraments as a particular community may celebrate, men are confronted by some aspect of the grace of God.

The Christian community's self-transcendence is affirmed by the reading and hearing of the "Word of God which is contained in the Scriptures of the Old and New Testaments," and by the careful teaching of it, whether from the pulpit, or in small face-to-face groups. The reading of Scripture in public worship originated as an act of teaching both in Jewish synagogue worship and in the Christian service. The teaching was in this instance first of all a confronting of the community by the Word of God. Thus it is of the genius of both the Jewish and the Christian community to embed teaching in the corporate worship of the community.

The self-transcendence of the Christian community is affirmed again by singing. Even the so-called subjective hymns, self-searching as they are, affirm that one searches himself in the Presence. But more yet the great "objective" hymns of the church affirm God in adoration, thanksgiving, joy. And the great music of the church affirms it, especially when virtuosity and self-display are put behind the back while instruments and voices make one great harmony from uplifted hearts.

Once more, the self-transcendence of the particular Christian community is affirmed whenever that community links itself in any manner, by thought or action, with the wider community, the holy catholic or universal church. The evidences of the self-transcendent nature of the Christian community might be adduced at still greater length. But the sum of the matter as far as self-transcendence is concerned may be expressed in this way: *The Christian community by virtue of its own nature is in the unique position of being a true community of living persons, but of being able also at the same time to stand above itself and view itself under the light of revelation and eternity.*

As a little band of men, women, and children they know and
affirm that they participate in that innumerable company of persons in all times and places who, in being found by God who is altogether worthy of supreme devotion, have begun to find themselves. And they are never more truly *themselves* than when they
affirm him in the triumphant hallelujahs of Christian faith.

In the second place this scene of a community which transcends itself in a *koinonia* with God is precisely the scene into
which men come bearing the intimate personal concerns of daily
life. As has so often been pointed out, it is only after we have first
made the affirmation of God by praying,

> Our Father who art in heaven, hallowed be thy name.
> Thy kingdom come.
> Thy will be done in earth as it is in heaven,

that we are ready in spirit to pray,

> Give us this day our daily bread.
> And forgive us our debts, as we forgive our debtors.
> And lead us not into temptation, but deliver us from evil.

Having so prayed, the community in its corporate prayer can then
again affirm its transcendent dimension:

> For thine is the kingdom, and the power, and the glory,
> forever. Amen.

For the Christian community, which is a self-transcendent
community, is at the same time a community of the concerned.
And what are the concerns it carries within itself? Exactly those of
which we have spoken in the first two chapters; these or any others
which go down to the roots of man's finite existence, or any such
as spring up out of them.

If we are members of a family we come, or we may come, as a
family group. This may be literally and physically true, as when
we sit together. But in a larger sense it may always be true, no matter what has happened physically to the family group. Spiritually
no one ever enters the sanctuary alone. He is always surrounded
and accompanied by all whom he has ever loved, whether they are

still counted among the living or have joined the greater assembly of the undying.

Into the worshiping community we come in our anxiety. We come, it may well be, frankly and unashamedly concerned over our own inward situation. It is our right to come in this concern, for who is to say that this was not the first reason we were called out to come? We come, too, equally and it may be much more concerned over those with whom our lives are knit together. There are great spiritual utterances in which a man prays to God that if any of his beloved people are to be blotted out, he may be blotted out with them.

We come concerned to know whether there is hope; not hope in the abstract, but hope for *us*, hope for *me*, hope for our time and for our world. It is to this concern to know whether there is hope, that the Christian gospel is addressed.

We come concerned over our relationships—to God, to other men, to oneself. To this concern, to say it again, the gospel is a proclamation of hope. The gospel is the affirmation, proclaimed as good news, that even as Jesus Christ died and rose again from the dead, so may we be raised up, now in the present hour, from our deadness to walk in newness of life.

Further, we come knowing well enough that in coming we shall be challenged as to our own responsibility as a community and as individuals. We have many forms of concern about this responsibility; as, for example, an apprehensiveness that others will press upon us a concern which we cannot feel; or an apprehensiveness that the concern which others feel will not match our own in intensity; or perhaps an apprehensiveness because we feel no concern, or because we feel our own concern too deeply as if one finite creature were taking upon himself all the burdens of the world.

A sense of corporate responsibility commonly characterizes the Christian community. This may be a sense of responsibility for the living or the well-being of its own members. It may be a sense of responsibility for reaching out in any of many ways beyond itself, notably in evangelistic and missionary effort, and in specific tasks of amelioration and reform. Thus whenever human selfhood is encroached upon, threatened, undermined, men commonly sense with sure intuition that this is a concern of the Christian community, or is due to be. They may fight back savagely at the church if they feel that *it* is encroaching upon *them* with its claims for human justice. Yet they know that if the church feels no concern it is not only a traitor to the society in which it exists, but a traitor to itself.

The fact that this sense of corporate responsibility tends to exist in some form and to some degree wherever the church exists partly accounts for the further accompanying fact that the church is a sort of embodied conscience within the social body. As such it stands as a threat to many. Some of these are persons who have had to free themselves from a morbid conscience based on some kind of idealized image. They believe that religion as they knew it contributed to morbidity, and they wish no more of it.

Wherever this feeling is well founded, such persons stand as a living reproach to any Christian community which, in offering salvation, succeeded only in putting men into a bondage which they could escape only by escaping the church. Some, however, to whom the church stands as a threat in the conscience are persons to whom any reminder of man's spiritual nature is an unwelcome reminder of a presently unspiritual existence which they have no desire to forsake.

At its best, in exercising its great function of moral reminder the church stands in the midst of the City of Man and calls upon it to become the City of God. At its best, too, this is no crying out of "holier than thou." For living in the midst of a disordered society in which it participates, it transcends itself by its prophetic word to itself and to the people of its day, speaking forth concerning men's sin and calling for repentance.

In the third place, not only does the Christian community transcend itself and bring its own profoundest concerns in to the place of meeting with God; it also knows that there is splitness within itself. Its people know there are rifts in the church, very deep rifts which neither the grace of God nor the passing of time has healed. Its people, knowing this, know that wholeness is not yet in the church itself.

This splitness exists between branch and branch of the church;

it exists between the particular Christian community and its neighboring Christian community, and sometimes within a particular community which is divided into factions. It often exists within one denomination, as when such a body is rent by controversy.

Splitness has led, of course, to every conceivable kind of conflict: to wars of religion, to inquisitions of many sorts in which Christians persecute Christians, and to the laying of rival religious claims before the civil courts for adjudication. And it has divided the church into denominations competing with one another for members, for territory, for privilege, for prestige, and for power.

The people of the churches are intensely aware of the rifts which divide the Christian church. Some regard it with incredulity and shame. Some hold to the division in a state of mingled conviction and regret. But some make their own persisting in division a matter of pride, because of what one's own branch of the church has meant in history. All these are ambivalent feelings, in which the possibility of repentance and reconciliation lies near the surface.

But there are those in whom this form of repentance seems impossible. Assured that they participate in the only true church, they assign places of spiritual peril to all outside it. And all this, being observed by the people who are outside the church, is understood clearly by them to be scandal, a stumblingblock.

Yet this is by no means all there is to say about the splitness of the church. For within the present century a prolonged and remarkable ecumenical movement has been under way, representing the effort from within the church to heal these divisions. This movement has expressed itself in a long series of unions between large denominations in Canada; and in the United States where the fragmenting of the church has proceeded to an extreme degree. Similar unions have taken place in many other lands.

The ecumenical movement is not merely on a national scale, but on one that is worldwide. The story is far too long to recount here, but for instance the Oxford and Edinburgh conferences of 1937, and the meeting of the World Council of Churches at Amsterdam in 1948, stand as monuments of spiritual yearning and striving on both sides of the Second World War.

So also in the United States the formation in 1908 of the Federal Council of the Churches of Christ in America, and of its successor the National Council of Churches, represent the springing up of the federal principle in lieu of deeper unity, before and after participation in world conflict. Many see in the ecumenical movement an inflow of the Spirit into the church at the very time when the demonic passion for destruction threatens to mount to proportions of global suicide.

Nevertheless one cannot study the church in history nor experience it as a living community in the present without having to admit that the existing church carries within itself powers both of a spiritual and of a demonic kind. It carries spiritual power which makes for the redemption and wholeness of the human self, of the church, and of society. But it also carries demonic power because men as human creatures carry potentially demonic power within themselves, and it is human creatures who make up the Christian community.

If any should flinch from the term "demonic" to denote any element or power within man, we ask only that he look at the toll of death and destruction wrought by man upon man in the present century and find for himself a more fitting term to denote the driving force of the passions let loose. Men with the capacity for this destructive power can unleash it in the name of God just as they can in the name of the state. Is it too much to say that there is that within a man which often secretly longs for a God who will command him to destroy?

But always in facing the demonic and destructive element which is so intertwined with the spiritual redemptive, we are brought back to the fact that the Christian community is a worshiping community. When we say that, we are also saying that in deliberately coming to meet with God man is coming to be met by God. There into the meeting place we come in anxiety and come also, it may be, to place our claims upon God and enlist him, as it were, to sit beside us to furnish the power and pay the tolls as we drive the car of our own destiny. But there in that same meeting place we are met by One who confronts us with *his* claims upon *us* and our living. We come asking from out of the framework of one dimension which is within us. But we are spoken to in the framework of another dimension which is also within us. Our responses make up the destiny which we choose.

But this is the story of revelation and encounter, into which we are to inquire more closely in later chapters. Here it must be enough to say that when the human self, whatever its brokenness and sin, comes to the place of meeting it is to be met by another Self who is within and yet beyond the human self. And in affirming God within that encounter, man is not only affirming Another. He is also affirming that which is at once the deepest and the highest that *he* is. He is affirming his life, but it is his eternal life which he is affirming. And he is affirming that it is not merely his duty, but rather his right, to live *now* in that dimension.

FORMAL ASPECTS OF THE CHURCH

In its formal aspects as an institution, the Christian church presents great variety; for example in polity, in forms of worship, in the conception of the clergy and their role, in the conception of the nature and efficacy of the sacraments, in credal formulas, and in the forms of piety which are cultivated in the people. Naturally they vary equally in the way church affairs are conducted, and in the subtle "feel" of the relationships which characterize the local communities of a particular branch of the universal church.

To take up subjects of such magnitude as these with any degree of carefulness is a vast study in itself,[5] and, however important such matters are in their own right, to pursue them here would divert us from the chief concerns that engage us in this book. We shall therefore have to restrict ourselves to a brief consideration of three formal aspects of the life of the local Christian community; namely, the offices of the church, the customs of the church, and the leadership of the church.

First, then, the offices of the church. In recent years many ministers and many who work in any capacity in the field of practical theology have been concerned over the fragmenting of the church's work, and therefore of its impact upon human life. They found a situation in which each phase of the church's work was tending to be lifted up into a specialty, assiduously cultivated, and made into an end in itself.

This situation represented a groping for a sense of relevance and practicality, especially in the American churches. It was a characteristically American way of trying to regain contact between the church and the people. Europeans find it hard to understand this phenomenon, and tend to discount it as mere activism, which of course it often is. But there is far more than mere activism in this phenomenon. It was a way of trying to avoid a deep peril. For Europeans who think lightly of activism apparently find it easy to forget that when a comparable distance between church and people has arisen in Europe, the discontent thus generated has often become one of the driving forces leading to revolution, and that in these revolutions the people often try to disestablish or even destroy the institution which has become irrelevant.

The feeling of distance between people and church had begun to assume large proportions in the United States by about the opening of the present century. In so far as this existed, it seems to have been part of a still wider sense of irrelevance concerning many, perhaps all, social institutions. Commager, for example, finds that a sense of irrelevance pervaded the feeling of people toward law, toward business, and toward government, as well as toward the churches.[6] Stringfellow Barr, in similar vein, shows that the high days of the cult of progress, from about 1870 to 1914, was the very time when a deep sense of man's estrangement from his own world was spreading insidiously both in Europe and in America.[7]

The feeling of alienation was reflected in numerous forms of expression, such as art, poetry, drama, fiction. It was reflected again in muckraking, exposure of scandal, debunking, and in numerous movements for reform.[8] Men were being alienated from their own culture because they felt it to be in so large a degree irrelevant to life as they knew it. But a countertide of quest for relevance in institutional life set in. The churches felt it, as did law, business, and government. This, we believe, is the larger source out of which the American churches' drive for practicality has come. It is in its deeper aspect a search for relevance.[9]

But if so, no one can doubt that this quest has often degenerated into a mere busy-ness, an activism for activity's sake. As the activities move further and further out to the periphery of the profoundest human concern, and further away from a rootage in a *worshiping* community, they lose the sense of being a continuum of the encounter with God. Then a fresh sense of irrelevance starts up. Losing a center from which they spontaneously spring, the activities must draw their inspiration from, and find their models in, secular life. Soon little or nothing is left to distinguish them from other legitimate secular activities.

The result, as far as the formal aspects of the church's work are concerned, was an increase of specialization in the ministry and in the curricula of the theological schools.[10] Each of those specializations was in some area of legitimate new concern or some area of familiar but almost forgotten concern. Hence each was in an area of some skill needed in the church's work. But the process of specialization itself reached such proportions, and drew off the energy of clergy and people to so many areas of such relatively minor concern, as to constitute a new and unintended threat to the integrity and wholeness of the church.

In the effort to find, not merely a present corrective, but a correcting principle for this state of things, a number of professors of practical theology under the leadership of Seward Hiltner, Oren H. Baker, and Otis R. Rice began to look at the deeper end of the question and ask what the offices or functions of *the church* truly are. It was an effort to recapture wholeness in the interaction between people in the worshiping community. As such there can be no doubt that their effort was inspired by the ecumenical movement. In a series of conferences these men came to the conclusion that the offices of the church as a worshiping community are:[11]

> Worship
> Preaching
> Education
> Pastoral Care
> Outreach; as in evangelism, missions, and
>   social action
> Administration

If this analysis is regarded as sound, then it would follow that each Christian community owes to its people each of these offices.

For each office represents some function of the community as a whole in relation to its own people, to the wider social community in which it is set, and to still others who live far out beyond that locale. And if the analysis turns out to need correction, these men will at least have suggested a point of beginning and a method of search, in the effort to attain wholeness in the life of the particular Christian community.

Second, there are the customs of the particular Christian community. Here we have in view the fact that each community has its own way of determining what the offices of that community shall be, discharging those offices, and putting into the discharging of them just that content and meaning which that particular community regards as most relevant to the situation of the people who comprise the community. This becomes a matter of making and administering policy. And again the numerous questions of practical import which arise cannot be pursued here. However, three points of especial significance need to be explicitly stated.

One is the fact that the particular community, because of institutional inertia, tends to respond slowly and cautiously to innovations in its customs. This has its good side, of course; otherwise the church would be led aside more often even than it is into chasing some will o' the wisp. But it means also that when a community has grown becalmed in its own traditions, or has allowed itself to be warped aside by inept steering into some small backwater of concern, it then requires leadership of exceptional ability to bring it out again into the great main current of the church's life and work.

A second point has to do with administration. The various offices of the church can be so administered as to bring them all into a full unity, thus furthering the sense of wholeness in the functioning of the total community. But, on the contrary, they may be so administered as to leave the various offices of the church more or less severed from one another, thus forming a splitness in functioning.

A third point has to do with a sense of belonging, so far as this depends upon the formal customs of the particular community. A sense of belonging within the Christian community can be fostered within the very young, whatever the theological position and the sacramental customs of the particular community. Indeed, a corrective seems to be needed as an accompaniment of *any* theological view of the formal place of children in the church.

For example, those communities which practice infant baptism, and those that practice both infant baptism and confirmation, seem commonly to face the possibility that these potentially rich rites will degenerate into meaningless acts. And those communities in which formal membership is withheld until formal profession of faith and baptism seem commonly to find that the rich meaning which underlies this custom may result in children's feeling that they are being shut out from that to which they wish to belong.

There is now a third formal aspect of the church's work to be brought into view; namely, leadership.[12] Leadership is a function of the relationship between persons, or of the relationships between an individual and a group. Saying that leadership is a function of relationships means that the *fact* of leadership exists *because* there are relationships which permit it or call for it. And it means that the *quality and results* of leadership depend upon the nature of the relationships existing between the persons involved. We may examine these points briefly.

In the Christian community there are certain formal positions in which persons are placed in the expectation that they will discharge leadership within and on behalf of the whole community. This includes, of course, all positions to which either men or women are ordained. But beyond this there is a wide range of other positions, more or less formal in nature and of longer or shorter duration, in which either men or women are placed in the expectation that they will exercise leadership among their own people. And still beyond is a sort of natural, informal leadership which often emerges during interaction within a group.

It should be emphasized, however, that leadership, whether in a formal or in an informal status, is both expected, and to a certain degree resented, by the members of a community. It is expected for obvious reasons. Without it, people feel "leaderless," as they say. They may grow confused, uncertain, and quickly come to feel that the community as such is beginning to disintegrate. But at the same time they are ready to resent leadership in so far as it suggests that they are not as capable as the leader, or whenever a leader begins to put pressure on them or threatens them; or whenever he disregards their situation, their needs, and their desires.

Thus the leader is very likely to arouse ambivalent feelings in those for whom he undertakes a responsibility. The positive feeling toward him is readily expressed by enthusiasm for him and responsiveness to him, and is witnessed to by more or less tangible results. The negative feelings which he arouses can be more readily expressed under some forms of polity than under others. But in any case they can accumulate underground until they explode under him with dismaying strength, perhaps at the very time when he supposes all is well.

All such considerations bring us to recognize that the leader's own inward situation as a self is quickly reflected in his leadership, by the kind of reaction he calls forth from other persons in his interaction with them. His own character situation as a person underlies his work and conditions its results. It is equally true, of course, that the character structures of the other persons in the community or the group condition *their* interaction with one another and with the leader. But at the moment we are thinking of the leader and his own inward situation.

The primary requisite for leadership, then, is a sound, healthy character structure which makes it possible for one to affirm the self-hood and well-being of others. Without this, the leader interacts less than helpfully, and perhaps damagingly, with other persons.

But the relationships between leader and led may be truly redemptive in their nature and in the end to which they lead in the Christian community. What is possible in this creative interaction is illustrated by another passage written by the same young man, quoted in the preceding chapter, who described himself as a prisoner to his own idealized image of himself. He writes:

One day I met a Man who let me be, not what I was, but what I am, and in that moment I became. He did not say I had to be this or that. He simply said, "Let's be." No fingers pointed, no demanding, staring eyes. Just he—and through him, let me be. I did not have to love, or do, or even be. Suffice to say, he just let me be. "You mean I do not *have* to walk the path?" "Why don't I have to walk it?" There! I've asked the question "why" and now the spell is broken. Now "whys" come tumbling all around. . . . What matters most is trusting where you put your feet, to feel a certain sureness that the world and you are not completely out of step . . . a new creation is in the process there—renewal of myself. And I am sure that it is good, for all the world takes on a newness.[13]

As one reads this account he cannot determine from the context which of two meanings is intended. Is this one-time "prisoner" saying that he met another man like himself, only more experienced in the ways of the spirit? Or is he saying that he met "the Man Christ Jesus"? Either of these is possible in the Christian community. Either meeting might mark the beginning of liberation.

CHAPTER IV

Within the Encounter

THE CHRISTIAN COMMUNITY, as other communities, is a body of relationships which carry both constructive and destructive forces.
But the Christian community is a self-transcending community;
and in the Christian community, as in no other community, the
fact of revelation faces us. This means that corrective, redemptive,
and re-creative power is forthgoing into the Christian community,
to reinforce the constructive forces which are at work, and to overcome other forces in the human self and in human relations which
are contrary to it.

If this is held to be true, all the offices of the church, from
worship to administration, will be affected by the fact of revelation, and will derive their own distinctive nature and their own
distinctive manner of functioning from it. This will be true in education, of course, just as in all the other offices of the church; and
education is the office of the church which is especially singled out
now for consideration.

How, then, is the "fact of revelation" to be understood, and
what is the relation between revelation and education? What is the
nature of Christian education, and how does it differ from other
forms of education? What is the human response to revelation; and
can it be among the results of Christian education, or does it belong
in a dimension where education is irrelevant? These are the chief
questions in this chapter.

REVELATION AND EDUCATION

In its most general sense revelation means an unveiling, a disclosure, a showing forth, of something. When the word is used in

its religious sense it is commonly understood to refer to a disclosure of God, as if to say that God has drawn away at least part of the veil which surrounds his Being.

The "fact of revelation" is the fact that an innumerable company of persons, from the most remote times to the present, have found themselves confronted by that which they have perceived as God disclosing himself. A report of revelation is the attempt to give an account of such an experience, in words which will so far as possible communicate to others what one has perceived when he was so confronted. A doctrine of revelation results when the reports of the original experiences are examined critically in the effort to determine whether the original experiences and the reports of them are authentic; and if they are authentic, to determine what they reveal, and what its relevance in the present is.

A report of revelation is not the revelation itself, but describes it and points to it. A doctrine of revelation is not even a report of revelation, but consists of propositions about revelation, built up after examining a mass of reports of revelation and drawing from them such generalizations as seem to be justified. A doctrine of revelation, then, certainly is not revelation itself, but is a generalization based on a mass of particulars.

A doctrine of revelation is also based in no small part on presuppositions which may not be contained in the reports of revelation. For example, if one is convinced on prior grounds that God is not Personal Being, the very term "revelation" itself will probably be an alien term coming out of a vocabulary which he cannot use with inward integrity; or at the most it will be a term which he is obliged to smooth down so that it will fit into presuppositions as to the way in which the power of the universe functions.

A doctrine of revelation thus is not only a body of generalizations based upon original experiences, but a body of changing generalizations. Even where the mass of underlying original experience is regarded as authentic, the generalizations based upon those original experiences have to be corrected and restated with the passing of generations. And where new knowledge throws new light upon the nature of the original experiences, the presuppositions with which one examines the reports of revelation are also subject to great shifts of change.

Thus it comes about that the doctrine of revelation is somewhat like the rising and receding of a tide in the life of the church. At times it recedes very far into the background, becoming obscured by all sorts of other concerns. At other times it rises in importance until it sweeps in upon the minds of men with such new force as to constitute almost a new revelation in itself. In our time the church is much nearer to this latter state of mind than it is to the former. The fact of revelation has swept in again to confront us, and to require that we grapple again with the doctrine of revelation.

The reports of revelation are by no means confined to the Jewish-Christian stream of history, for the history of religion abounds in reports of encounter with God or with the gods. Moreover, in the Jewish-Christian stream reports of revelation are not confined to the Scriptures of the Old and New Testaments, for reports of revelation, which are not recorded in the Bible, were numerous in ancient times and new reports have continued to be made ever since.

This means that in the Christian church a great mass of reports of revelation has been tested and sifted out on the basis of a doctrine of revelation. As a result of this sifting, a certain number of books, which we now know as the books of the Bible, were chosen as "canonical," that is, suited for reading aloud in the worshiping community as uttering the Word of God for the teaching of the people.

Thus the reports of revelation with which the Christian community is primarily concerned are contained in the Bible. These reports of revelation presented to us as the Word of God face us whenever we come into the Christian community. At the same time our doctrine of revelation, whatever that doctrine may be in the present, is a body of propositions as to the way in which we on our part are to face the fact of revelation and the reports of revelation.

So in the Christian community there is, there has always been, and presumably there must always be, a tension between the fact of revelation and the reports of revelation on the one hand, and some doctrine of revelation on the other hand. It is as if the fact of revelation and the reports of revelation were constantly pressing in upon the minds of men in the Christian community. The doctrine of revelation represents, as it were, the frame of reference in our own minds as we prepare to hear and respond.

The doctrine of revelation therefore, from one point of view, is almost as important as the fact of revelation and the reports of revelation; because it has so much to do with what we shall hear and ask others to hear in the Christian community, and so much to do with determining the frame of mind with which we shall begin to respond and open or close the way for others to respond. The doctrine of revelation, then, is a crucial element in the life of the Christian community and in the philosophy of Christian education. Indeed, it could be maintained that it is the determinative element in both. That is to say, any philosophy of Christian education must incorporate a doctrine of revelation in *some* form or other.

The doctrine of revelation which is incorporated into a philosophy of Christian education can take a negative form. Many negative forms of the doctrine of revelation are possible. For example, if there is the presupposition that God can in no way be known and communicated with as Personal Being, the philosophy of Christian education must be constructed around that premise.

The doctrine of revelation as incorporated into the philosophy of Christian education can take a positive form. Again, many variations are possible. But, for example, if there is even so much as an openness of mind toward the possibility that God can be known and communicated with as Personal Being, a philosophy of Christian education can be constructed which is consistent with the doctrine of revelation as confrontation. This in turn would mean that the educational work of the Christian community could be carried on in such a way as to allow the fact of revelation and the reports of revelation to speak for themselves to the members of the Christian community. What, then, is meant by revelation as confrontation?

To express the concept of revelation as confrontation in one of the simplest ways possible would be to say that God as Self confronts man as a self, and has disclosed himself to man.

To speak thus of "confrontation" means that God as infinite Personal Being faces man as a finite personal being. In terms which we have used earlier, it implies that in any togetherness between God and man there is always also a separateness of selfhood. It implies that man is not himself a god, but faces God; and if in facing God he is drawn toward God he is not absorbed into God. But on the other hand it does *not* need to imply, as some would have it, that God as Personal Being is wholly outside man as a personal being; for the doctrine of the Spirit of God means that God as Personal Being is perceived as present within man as a personal being, present within man yet not identical with man.

To speak of revelation as God's *Self*-disclosure implies that *what* is revealed in the encounter between man and God is not information *about* God, but God *himself* as Personal Being. The reports of revelation may have to be cast in terms that contain information, or that attempt to describe what was perceived in the encounter. But in the encounter itself what is disclosed is some aspect of infinite, perfect Selfhood, being unveiled in some form of relationship with finite, imperfect selves.

To speak of revelation as confrontation implies, further, that human perception is involved in revelation. Revelation is revelation *to human beings*. The capacities of the human self are engaged in receiving what is communicated in revelation. This does not mean that no one benefits from revelation unless he knows he is doing so. It does mean that unless he *perceives* what is disclosed, the disclosure has not yet reached him. For to perceive is more than merely "seeing" what is manifested, and it is more than "hearing" what is uttered. One can see, and not perceive; one can hear, and not understand. Accordingly it is common to find that communication has broken through the confines of what a man already "knew."

After these general statements regarding revelation as confrontation, we may consider some of the more specific questions regarding the nature of revelation.

In the Biblical accounts of revelation there are various media through which God reveals himself to man, and where his disclosure of himself to man is perceived. These media are commonplace, in the sense that they are known, or may readily become known, to the members of the religious community. This means that a great part of God's disclosure of himself is made through what is already known.

Among the chief media employed for this purpose are physical nature, human nature, events in history[1] and, above all, Jesus Christ the living "Word of God," himself the culmination of revelation. The materials taken from such media provide symbols drawn from the realm of that which can be known by the senses. The symbols represent some aspect of God as Personal Being who cannot be fully known since he is infinite, but who yet can be truly known by the aid of the symbols. The symbol then in turn becomes a means of communication in the religious community regarding man's situation, and regarding the corrective, redemptive, and recreative power of God.

In the Bible, as just said, *physical nature* is a medium of revelation. This is especially prominent in the Old Testament, but it is not absent from the New Testament. The objects and the forces of the physical world are viewed in the Bible as created by God, deriving their nature from God, dependent upon God for their existence, and obedient to the will of God in their operation.[2]

Therefore in the Biblical view the things of nature, in what they are and in what they do, "speak" of God by manifesting his wisdom and power. From a vantage point of this kind, animals, birds, insects, reptiles, flowers, rivers, mountains, winds and clouds, rain and sunshine, and the heavenly bodies, to mention no others, all have something to show forth concerning God. The regularity of the seasons testifies to the dependability of God's covenant with man. The convulsive displays of power as in the storm and the earthquake, and the destruction wrought by drought and pestilence, are commonly perceived as messengers of God to express his judgment.

Again, *human nature* is viewed in the Bible as a medium of revelation. Indeed, it would be nearer accuracy to say that human nature is *experienced* as a medium of revelation. For man as a self has the capacity to answer to God as Self, and selfhood in man is experienced as a clue to the nature of Selfhood in God. To experience selfhood as man, within the limits of finiteness, is to experience the counterpart of Selfhood which is infinite. This, as was observed in the first chapter, is part of the meaning which lies in the concept that man is created in the image of God.

The anthropomorphisms which abound in the Bible express the vivid perception of personality in God. They lose their power to represent the depth of the Selfhood which confronts man, if the doctrine of revelation is allowed to demand that they be understood literally. They lose their power to represent the depth of the selfhood which is potentially in man, if the doctrine of revelation to demand that the anthropomorphic terms for God must be understood as a mere projection of human personality. They retain their power to represent depth in both these dimensions when they are understood as a Hebrew way of saying concretely something which a philosopher might prefer to say abstractly.

As the Biblical symbols representing God grow more spiritual and more reticent about "the body" of God, the marks of Selfhood in God are never lost. His self-consciousness as one who is "I," his will as one who not only determines but also communicates, and his character as one who both affirms and opposes man—these are never drained out in the Biblical reports of revelation. Instead, they stand forth with growing majesty in the deepening Self-disclosure which is "the fact of revelation."

Again, human nature is experienced as a medium of revelation, not only because selfhood in man is the counterpart of Selfhood which is in God, but also because there is that in the human self and in human relationships in which God is present, participant, and visible. In the Bible God is perceived as disclosing himself in great part through the commonplace which he indwells and affirms. It is good, not because it is extraordinary, but just because it is ordinary. So prominent is this element in Biblical revelation that William Temple could speak of "the sacramental view of the universe,"[3] in which the spiritual can be seen disclosed through the material. The common relationships of life and the common acts of the day are constantly being drawn upon to furnish symbols for some aspect of what God is and does.

As symbols they are not merely poetic figures of speech, although they often have great poetic beauty. The relationships and acts of the common life are symbols in the sense that they participate in that for which they stand. They do not merely suggest something else; they contain at least a part of what they stand for. To miss this is to miss a great core in revelation itself. Thus in the love of a father or mother for a child, in the love between husband and wife, in the love of brother for brother or friend for friend, in the breaking of bread, or in some other simple act which instantly wipes out a gulf of separateness between man and man, God is not merely suggested; he is disclosed, participant and visible to perception.

But this is not all that is revealed through human nature as a medium. In the Bible God confronts man not only as friend, but also as enemy. If there is that in human nature and in human relationships which he affirms, there also is that which he opposes. The nature of selfhood in God is disclosed by that which he opposes and rejects, as truly as by that which he affirms. That which he rejects is whatever springs out of the perversion or the corruption of man's freedom as a self, a community, or a nation.

Under both the Old Covenant and the New the question of obedience and disobedience to the specifics of the law is never allowed to remain long at the center of concern. Judgment finally is judgment not upon the specifics of action as such. It finally is judgment upon the secret recesses of the self out of which the specifics of action spring. It is the secret places of that labyrinth underneath human action, the human will, which lie exposed to the light. Under that light the falsities, the pretensions, and the idolatries of self, community, and nation are "naked and opened unto the eyes of him with whom we have to do."[4]

The factor of divine opposition is as crucial in revelation as is the factor of the divine affirmation of man. It is God's perception of us which is being revealed for our perception both of him and of ourselves. Potentially it is the beginning of that phase of human self-understanding which a man cannot achieve for himself in isolation, but which can be given him in relationship with another. This double motion of affirming man and yet opposing him runs like warp and woof through the Biblical account of revelation, and comes to climax in the meaning which the writers of the New Testament perceive in the death and resurrection of Jesus Christ.

Still again, *events in history* are viewed in the Bible as a medium of revelation. The occurrences of nature, but especially the occurrences of human history, are saying something to man. Events comprise, as it were, a language by which communication takes place between the Creator and his creatures. In events God confronts man as Person confronts persons, and speaks through the events.

What is communicated through the events is *meaning in the events*. It is God who gives the meaning; that is to say, the events are not the bare so-called "facts of history"; they utter something. They disclose something of the character of God who acts in history to call, to judge, and to deliver.

And if it is God who gives the meaning which is disclosed through the events of history, it is man who perceives it; or rather, it is man who *may* perceive it. Thus, as William Temple expresses it, the essence of revelation consists of a living intercourse between mind and world-process, between mind and event. Event in this instance is the language of communication between Personality and personality; and revelation takes place when event and "appreciation" of the meaning of the event coincide.[5]

Appreciation, which is perceiving the meaning of the event or events of history, may come at the time of the event, or it may come later, or it may fail to come at all. The prophet is, among other things, one who "hears" what is spoken through event. He is a "seer" who perceives what is being uttered through event. He speaks forth for God when he seeks to communicate the meaning of the word of God which he has heard or seen.

A large part of the Bible is given over to telling of great revelatory events, and then retelling them from the vantage point of later history. This is because the original revelatory event can be reperceived with new and deeper meaning as time passes. Thus in Israel's history there are certain revelatory events of especial significance, such as the call of Abraham, the deliverance from bondage in Egypt, and the Babylonian captivity, which are remembered and freshly perceived, generation after generation.

Hence one of the great imperatives of the Jewish-Christian faith is "Remember!" But on the other hand those same great events were often forgotten by the people who, in forgetting, lost their sense of rootage in the covenant. Such forgetting was an event of primary significance in itself, for it constituted a repudiation of revelation. Hence one of the great recurring questions both in the Old Testament and in the New is, "Have you forgotten?"

Remembering and reperceiving bring meaning not only into the past, but into the present as well. For this is *our* history, and it brings meaning into *our* lives. This aspect of revelation leads Richard Niebuhr to speak of "appropriating" revelation, and he says:

By revelation in our history, then, we mean that special occasion which provides us with an image by means of which all the occasions of personal and common life become intelligible. What concerns us at this point is not the fact that the revelatory moment shines by its own light and is intelligible in itself but rather that it illuminates other events and enables us to understand them. Whatever else revelation means it does mean an event in our history which brings rationality and wholeness into the confused joys and sorrows of personal existence and allows us to discern order in the brawl of communal histories . . . the revelatory moment is revelatory because it is rational, because it makes the understanding of order and meaning in personal history possible.[6]

Revelation as understood in the Bible thus has the double quality of being rooted in the events of history and yet of being prolonged in history in such a way that the revelatory events of the past continue to disclose not a fixed and dead meaning, but a living God who still speaks freshly through what he has already said. This principle makes the history of the people of God a continuum, gives that history a basal place in Christian education, and puts one's own personal history in the great context of the history of redemption.

But above all other media of revelation, *God confronts man in Jesus Christ*. In him God's disclosure of himself to man comes to culmination. In him human nature as a medium of revelation and event as a medium of revelation coalesce into one supreme Word of God. It is this which permits Paul to say, "In him dwelleth all the fulness of the Godhead bodily."[7]

In his human nature men behold what man may become. Selfhood was complete; hence the frequent use of the term "fullness" in the New Testament. This denotes both the fullness of manhood, and the fullness of God which took up its dwelling in complete manhood. In the phrase we earlier used, in knowing himself he knew God and in knowing God he knew himself.

It is testified of him that he did not come by this fulfillment of manhood without struggle. When it is said that he was tempted, it is being asserted that he knew anxiety as other men do; but of his own will sought to know, and of his own will sought to keep to, the destiny for which he had been sent into the world. When it is said of him that he was without sin, it is being affirmed that in him sonship to God was complete, without alienation either from God or from himself. He could completely fulfill the destiny for which he had come into the world. To see this "fullness" was not merely to see a man; it was to see God. So it could be reported of him that he said, "He that hath seen me hath seen the Father."[8]

Hence he is himself the Word of God.[9] This means that in the last analysis the truth which God has communicated is not an oracle, not a proposition, not a doctrine, but a Person. Through him grace and truth *became* (*egeneto*), came into being. That is to say, both grace and truth are disclosed as a concrete, individual Person who can be seen, heard, handled, responded to.[10]

The Gospel of John is so constructed as to describe in symbols drawn from the common life what it means to encounter this living Word of God. To reject this Word is to live in darkness when we were created to live in light. It is to stand like Pilate facing the truth in person, yet in that very moment of encounter to keep on repeating the old, sterile intellectual question, "What is truth?"[11] But to those who "receive" the living Word he is light, water, bread; he is the shepherd, the door, the way; he is as the vine is to the branches; and above all he is life, even resurrection from the dead. To such as receive him he gives "power to become the sons of

God."[12] For they know the truth who is a person, and the truth who is a person has set them free.[13]

We have already said that revelation through human nature and revelation through the events of history coalesce into one supreme disclosure of God through Jesus Christ. The life itself taken as a whole is the revelatory event by which all other revelation must be oriented. But within the life as a whole there are two events which finally become the two foci for the deepest perception of God's Self-disclosure through Jesus Christ. These are his death and his resurrection.

Each of these, the death by crucifixion and the resurrection, was a scandal then as now. Each was incomprehensible on any commonly accepted basis of thinking. Each violated some structure of thought within which great numbers of men were seeking to live an orderly life.

His death was a scandal then for all who expected a Messiah. It required that they either regard him as a failure or a traitor, or else that they reinterpret virtually the whole of the sacred writings. And his death is a scandal now to all who put their faith in the goodness of men or in the self-rewarding virtues of the good life. For he had lived the perfect life, only to be done to death by the champions of God and the officers of the state.

But to talk of his resurrection from the dead, as his heralds did, was to raise a scandal of a more insidious kind. This was a thing that simply does not happen, and to claim that it had happened was to raise doubt about the sanity of the man who made the claim. It violated common sense to such a degree that some hearers walked out with a shrug, while others tapped the forehead in pity for the man who could talk such nonsense.

Yet it was upon precisely those two events that the central message, the gospel, rested. And why? It was because those men perceived what confronted them in these two events. They understood that the death and the resurrection were not merely two real historical events, one tragedy and the other triumph, transpiring in the body of Jesus Christ. These two events were more than that. They were events in which any man in any time or place might participate, and participating know in himself the love of God and the power of God as in no other way.

We have already observed that the double motion of affirming man and yet opposing man runs as a constantly recurring thread through the Biblical records of revelation. Like so much else, this comes to its climax in the meaning which faith perceived in Jesus Christ. The church has understood from the beginning that the death of Jesus Christ bore a double meaning; it was judgment upon man, yet it was sacrifice on behalf of man. It disclosed a relationship between God and man wherein divine judgment goes forth, yet is contained within the firm orbit of profound acceptance by God.

A relationship between man and God is thus disclosed wherein man can retreat still further from God, or can move in the core of his being toward God. In retreating still further from God he is not only widening the separation between himself and God; he is widening the rift within himself as a man. But in moving toward God he can begin to accept the divine judgment upon the hidden places of his own being in that deep change of mind which is called repentance. And he can begin to test God's acceptance of him by that profound forthgoing of the whole self in movement toward God which is called faith.

Within such an encounter the rift within man himself can be healed, so that in being reconciled with God he is reconciled with himself. In such a case a man has found himself in grasping Another who had already gone forth to meet him. He has not been over-powered; he has been empowered with the power to become what he is. In the New Testament it is perceived that this is participating in the resurrection of Jesus Christ. By faith a man participates both in the death and in the resurrection, not as some remote event, but as a present moment of redemption and re-creation of his own self.

All this and much more besides, the church has sought to express through its doctrines of incarnation and atonement. These doctrines, shifting in emphasis through the centuries, have not infrequently become a greater scandal for faith than the events of revelation upon which the doctrines were based. But the core of the matter is expressed in the Pauline saying, "God was in Christ, reconciling the world unto himself."[14] For "to reconcile" means to change thoroughly, to bring about change in the depth of the self and in its relationship to God.

But when all is said, this mystery of becoming in Christ Jesus what we were created to be cannot be captured in doctrinal phrases. It is witnessed to in the worshiping community. It is known in such experiences as the breaking up an old self which was like darkness and storm, and the emerging of new life that feels like the morning dawning. It is common for the reborn to say that everything looks different now. They understand what is meant by the saying, "Behold, I make all things new."[15] For one who is called the Son of Man has brought newness within, hence now all is also new around them.

It remains to state more explicitly two points of major importance which have been implicit throughout this discussion of revelation. One is that *revelation is redemptive in nature*. This is the point of contact between the subjects considered in the first two chapters, and the subject of revelation. The human self when living in anxiety and alienation is under threat to its very existence. The essence of revelation as God's Self-disclosure is the movement of the divine Self toward the human self, and the essence of the movement of the divine Self is its redemptive purpose.

The second major point now to be made still more explicit is that *the normal scene of revelation is the scene where fellowship exists*. As Self-disclosure, revelation involves encounter, the meeting between selves. In theory God may confront man and be perceived by man under any circumstances. But it appears that commonly he does confront men in circumstances where fellowship between man and man and between man and God already exist.

This means that the fellowship of the religious community is intended really to be a revelatory fellowship, both in Judaism and in Christianity. In the Old Testament the revelatory fellowship is the covenant. In the New Testament it is the *koinonia*.

If we seek to sum up all that has been said regarding the nature of revelation, one thing stands out above all others. It is that revelation takes place in the meeting between God as Person and man as a person. Revelation is not information about God; it is what happens in the encounter between God as Self and man as a self. It was so in the original revelation, and continues to be so as original revelation is prolonged into present time through its various media.

And now we are in search of a Christian education which is consistent with this core principle of revelation. What is the nature of such an education, and how does it differ from other forms of education? This is the second general question of the present chapter.

THE NATURE OF CHRISTIAN EDUCATION

Education in its broadest sense has to do with the changes which take place in persons. Many of the changes which take place are, of course, outside the scope of education in any useful sense of the term. But those changes that take place in the human being as he strives to attain selfhood constitute a field in which education can operate because these changes are affected by the interaction between persons. And this interaction is more or less subject to direction and control.

Society has a very high stake in these changes, or "learnings." For example, the character structure, the relationships, the realization of personal potentiality, and the manner of living of its members constitute the kind of stuff out of which a society is made or unmade. "Education" means that society in some manner participates in the striving of its members to attain selfhood. Education means further that society not only participates in that striving but seeks to guide it toward those ends which the society regards as most worthy.

It is common now to say that at least two kinds of education go on within society, the informal and the formal. A society carries on an informal education of its members, just by being what it is and seeking what it seeks as a society. This kind of education is unorganized, but powerful. By all that it does and does not do, by all that it values and disvalues, by what it rewards with its highest prizes and by what it penalizes by shutting people out from its best prizes, and in hundreds of other subtle ways a society infuses itself into its members.

A society also commonly carries on some kind of formal education. In this, the society undertakes deliberately to participate in the becoming of its members and to guide that becoming.

These general statements regarding the meaning of education in its broadest sense hold true whether education is conceived in secular or in religious terms. The fact of human interaction and the processes of human interaction are for all practical purposes the same in each. The principal differences between the secular and the religious conceptions of education lie, we propose, in three areas.

There is first the nature of the educating society. In the case of a secular community the educating society is the state, or some segment of it. The state is in some sense sovereign. At least in its internal affairs it recognizes no sanction from beyond itself, and hence has no corrective for itself except such as springs up from within itself. And the state imposes its will upon the secular community by determining that there shall be a system of education, determining by authority what that system of education shall be, and compelling by law that the young shall go to school.

In the case of the Christian community the educating society is the Christian community itself. It acknowledges a sovereignty which is above that of the state. Since it faces the fact of revelation, it operates under conditions which not only permit but call for a constant corrective of itself from beyond itself. And in the United States, as in many other lands, the church is not established by law; membership in it is voluntary, and attendance upon its schools is voluntary. In view of these differences between the educating societies, the charge of "authoritarianism in education" which is sometimes directed at the modern church sounds a little hollow.

A second area of difference between the secular and the Christian societies in education has to do with those who are avowed to be participant in education. In the case of secular education the avowed participants are human beings interacting in natural processes. In the case of Christian education the avowed participants also are, of course, human beings interacting in natural processes. But beyond that it is further avowed that God is participant in the community; and that the processes of interaction are capable of carrying a corrective, redemptive, and re-creative power which comes in from beyond purely natural processes, not violating those processes nor setting them aside, but able to transform them. In short it is avowed that in the Christian community God is participant, not merely in processes but in acts, disclosing himself in revelation and imparting himself in grace.

A third area of difference between the secular society and the Christian community has to do with the ends sought by participating in, and attempting to guide, the changes which take place in persons. In both forms of society much effort has gone into the attempt to define the ends of education, and in both there is great variation in the resulting statements of ends.[16]

In both secular and Christian education there has arisen a certain degree of sympathy with the view that there is no "end" at all in education except such as exists within the process of interaction itself. In this view the processes of interaction can be so refined by human intelligence as to become redemptive. But such a view takes no adequate account of the demonic element in human interaction, nor of the demonic purposes to which intelligence in interaction can be turned. Hence in the midst of the twentieth century the view seems generally being rejected, at least to the extent that both secular and religious societies frankly assume the heavy burden of defining the ends sought in education.

In the case of the secular society the ends sought seem now commonly to be put in terms of well-being as an individual, worthy membership in society, and worthy citizenship in the state. However, in regard to the last point the American people at the present writing are witnessing a new outburst of secular witch-hunting, secular heresy trials, and legally protected slander of allegedly disloyal persons, reaching into every level of educational work. It is being conducted to a large degree by one branch of the national government. It is the kind of phenomenon which we have long associated with the church and with totalitarian countries elsewhere, but supposed we had put behind forever. Whatever else it may mean by the time the story has run its course, it deserves to be remembered as an exhibit of what the sovereignty of the state can become overnight, in setting the ends of education.

In the case of the Christian community the ends sought have also been stated with great variation; but they seem commonly to turn in some manner upon the development of the self, worthy citizenship in the kingdom of God, and worthy membership in society.

The great differences in the ends sought by the secular community and those sought by the Christian community, however, lie not merely in the statement of ends, but in the differing concepts of the nature of the human self, in the differing concepts of the nature and obligations of membership in human society, and above all in regard to the concept of the sovereignty of God over men and nations.

The common Christian understanding is that Jesus Christ is "the way" by which men may enter into the kingdom of God and thus come under the sovereignty of God. Thus the Christian community knows a sovereignty which is above all other sovereignties, and knows "the way" which is above all other ways into the realm of that sovereignty. Our liberty to believe this and to avow it is held at the price of living as subjects of a civil state which as state cannot believe this nor avow it, and hence cannot teach it. But no Protestant would willingly have it otherwise if he understands his own heritage as American Protestant. For in this provision he finds civil protection of two great spiritual rights of man: the right to place the sovereignty of God above every other sovereignty, and the right to stand fully within the state as subject to it and yet the right to stand above it and view it as under judgment just as he himself and his Christian community are.

If then it is asked what Christian education is, it is suggested that a statement of its nature would include such terms as these: *Christian education is the attempt, ordinarily by members of the Christian community, to participate in and to guide the changes which take place in persons in their relationships with God, with the church, with other persons, with the physical world, and with oneself.*

In such a conception of Christian education the *scene* of Christian education is the Christian community as a *koinonia* in which both men and God participate in an intricate web of relationships. The *koinonia* exists in the household quite as truly as it does in the church. But always in the *koinonia*, by virtue of its own nature, it is understood and avowed that God is participant.

In the *koinonia* there are two poles or foci; namely, man and God. The two encounter each other and interact with each other so that they are drawn together or draw further apart according to the nature of the relationship set up between them during the encounter.

A statement of the *ends sought* in Christian education might contain such elements as these: that persons might be drawn into the kingdom of God; that they might attain to increasing self-understanding and self-knowledge and an increasing realization of their own potentialities; and that they might sustain the relationships and responsibilities of life as children of God.

Such a statement of ends sought, cast as it is in terms that are so general, is in contrast with statements of highly specific "outcomes." It is intended to be so. For the more specific the aims become, the more surely are we drawn into the business of trying to predetermine for others what their behavior and what their feelings should be; and then accordingly the more inevitably are we drawn into manipulating them to make this come true. How are we then to avoid the opposite and rejected extreme of adopting an education which professes to have no aim outside the process of interaction itself?

To avoid both perils means keeping the situation of the presently existing self at the center of concern. And it means that the principal changes which are the subject of concern are changes in the depths of the self instead of those which are at the periphery of the self. Here the concept of revelation as confrontation takes on especial significance for Christian education.

For when man encounters the Self-revealing God he is confronted, not by a release of fresh divine information to be digested, not by some new and infallible dogma about God, not by a list of new rules to be observed or old ones to be furbished up again; he is confronted by none of these trappings of religion and churchcraft, but by a Person who offers himself to us in love and in judgment, and calls upon us to give ourselves a living sacrifice in response. It is a matter of personal communion. If this is the core of revelation, so must it be the core of Christian education.

In Christian education so conceived, the changes that take place in the depths of the self are of concern not only to the one in whom they take place, but to God as well. Often these changes are in the nature of movement in the self in a struggle for life and against death. In such a struggle God is concerned. To that assertion revelation constantly testifies. In Christian education we are given the opportunity to participate with one another in that encounter wherein God goes forth to meet the soul struggling for its own existence.

How do we get any inkling of the deeper anxieties, concerns, and tensions which exist beneath the surface of the interaction which is taking place? In the most general terms it can be said that we disclose it to one another *by communication*. This is not to say that we really discover ourselves to one another by talking back and forth; quite as likely we hide ourselves as well as we can under those conditions. Nor does it mean sending messages across the air over a few feet of space or over leagues of it.

All of these are means of communication, of course. But the deeper communication we now have in view is the opening of two or more selves to one another at deeper and deeper levels, in an unthreatening atmosphere, until what each wants to say and hardly dares to say can be expressed and made common between two selves, or between all the selves. "Communication is a balsam which heals the wounds acquired in the battle for life."[17] It is between man and man what revelation is between God and man—self-disclosure to one who can perceive and respond.

Any genuine struggle for redemption and wholeness produces a body of symbols. This body of symbols, whether private to one person or common to many, is a potential means of communication whereby one person may interpret to another person the meaning of *his* search for redemption and re-creation.

One of the marks which distinguish communication in the Christian community from other forms of communication is the fact that the Christian church holds in common *an extraordinarily rich body of symbols for communication* regarding the anxieties, the concerns, the tensions, the relationships, and the interaction of human existence, and the divine response through revelation and through grace, to these concerns of human life.

This rich body of materials for communication can be so used as to serve a threefold purpose: to facilitate communication at a deeper level regarding our deeper human concerns; to give an otherwise lonely struggler a sense of participating with countless others who have striven as he must strive in the issue between life and death; and to quicken his ability to perceive that he in his present hour is being grasped by the corrective, redemptive, and re-creative power of God.

It may be said, then, that *the means to the ends sought* in Christian education are such as: introducing persons to the Christian community, introducing them to the Bible and the Christian heritage, preparing the way for personal response to revelation, participating with them in purposeful action, and counseling with them during periods of crisis.

As to *processes of interaction*, communication requires a two-way current of interaction between persons; namely, an educing and an imparting. Eduction is the leading out, the leading forth or calling forth of one self by another self. Impartation is the giving forth of at least a part of one self who is in communication with another. It is putting some part of the self or even all of the self into the keeping of another so that the two have this much in common between them.

This two-way current of interaction can degenerate. Eduction when it degenerates becomes manipulation, in which persons are treated as things, and then must be persuaded if possible that the manipulation is for their own good. As impartation degenerates it offers something else as a substitute for the giving forth of a self. Thus for example impartation may degenerate into transmitting inert "materials" from one person to another without any significant communication ever taking place between them.

But in the Christian community when deeper communication is taking place, both eduction and impartation mean that there is a profound encounter between self and self within a field of concern in which God as forthgoing Spirit is participant. And this is a two-way current, because in deep communication all parties to the encounter are called out and drawn forth, while at the same time all parties to the encounter go forth from within themselves and give forth out of themselves.

Accordingly, in the profoundest communication the interaction which takes place is nothing less than the interpenetration of selves into one another.

THE RESPONSE TO REVELATION

What is the nature of the human response to revelation? Can it be among the results of Christian education, or does it belong in a dimension where education is irrelevant?

If revelation is God's Self-disclosure to man, then the core of the result, looked at from the human side, is to be found in the response of the human self to the divine Self, God. It is a matter between person and Person, between an I and a Thou.

The human response to revelation may be either negative or positive. The negative response is the rejection of the divine Self by the human self. It is a refusal in some form to be drawn into a self-to-Self relationship of mutual self-giving. In Biblical language this negative response is described in such terms as hearing God and refusing to answer, seeing light but refusing to acknowledge its meaning or refusing to follow it; knowing God and then forgetting him, hardening the heart, rebelling, and many others. It is man's "No" to God.

In its positive form the human response to revelation is as simple as, and yet more complex than, the "Yes" which we utter in the deepest moments of our human relationships. It is the "Yes" of the human self to the divine Self who is disclosing himself. When the positive response is put in terms of believing, having faith, and the like, the verbs and prepositions commonly suggest movement of the whole self toward or into God. When it is put in terms of man's affirmation of God's revelation, it is expressed by the "Amen," which is a positive assertion: "So be it." When it is put in terms of obedience it is expressed by action, doing the will of God.

We have to reckon both with the response to original revelation and with the response to dependent or derived revelation, which some prefer to call illumination. The Bible contains records of original revelation and records of the human response to that revelation. It is thus a witness both to original revelation and to original responses to that revelation.

Later human response to original revelation is possible, in principle, at any time. It is possible, for example, whenever any person feels that some original Self-disclosure of God is relevant to his present situation. It is possible also whenever any person feels that some original human response to original revelation is the response which he, man in the present moment, needs or desires to make. Similarly, in principle the response to dependent revelation is possible for any person in any moment of personal history.

The possibility of continuing divine Self-disclosure is Biblically expressed in terms of the Spirit of God. As has been said earlier, "the Spirit of God" is literally the "wind" or "breath" of God. The symbol represents the forthgoing of the divine Self into the world but especially into the human self. It represents in the divine-human relationship a kind of encounter analogous to the interpenetration which we have already seen in the interaction between human selves. Biblically this is expressed by sometimes saying that the Spirit is in man, and sometimes saying that man is in the Spirit. In either case it is a time of intimate nearness, of illumination, of assurance, and of power imparted and received.

Furthermore, when the Spirit is described as going forth into the human scene, very often the point of the account is that the divine Self-disclosure precisely fits some particular human situation or need. Many of the classic terms used to describe the activity of the Spirit of God in relation to man denote an intensely personal encounter. Thus the Spirit is sent or goes forth to some one individual as well as into the Christian community. The Word of God is addressed to some one person as well as to the community. What characterized the tongues of fire at Pentecost was the fact that every man could hear the Spiritual utterance in his own language. There is a rich array of terms to describe the continuing Self-disclosure of God to man.

We have next to inquire into the relation between divine initiative such as is implied in the "confrontation," and human initiative such as is implied in the term "education." We should say parenthetically that while there is variation in the usage, the term "confrontation" may be taken as implying *divine* initiative and activity, as when it is said, "God confronts man"; while the term "encounter" may be taken as representing the experience of being confronted. Now if revelation is confrontation, and if confrontation implies divine initiative, we are obliged to ask whether there can be any human participation in the encounter with God except the direct response of the individual person who has been confronted.

In a word, if one believes in revelation can he give any place at all to education? More specifically, if revelation means that God discloses himself to man, *can* one person participate in bringing about the encounter between some other person and God, or must he wait for God to act? *Can* one participate in and help to guide the changes taking place in some other person's relationship to God, or are such changes something which only God can bring about?

Confrontation can be so interpreted as to exalt the divine initiative and depreciate human initiative until virtually no room is left for the latter. There is then little or no place for human participation in bringing about the encounter between man and God. The result is a more or less extensive paralysis of will. Recognition of the necessity for personal decision dwindles. Moral effort on behalf of others begins to be regarded as meddling in the secret counsels of the Most High. It is a religious form of determinism, the more insidious when it invades the religious community because it has so much to say about giving God the glory.

This general view of confrontation has taken many specific forms, some ancient and some modern. Various forms of the doctrine agree in regarding the efforts of parents and teachers to bring about the encounter with God as being irrelevant to say the least, and possibly harmful or even blasphemous. Such doctrines are commonly thought of as being hostile to Christian education; and in a sense this is true enough, of course.

It should be observed, however, that we are actually dealing here with certain forms of the doctrine of revelation which in turn underlie corresponding forms of Christian education. The fact that these forms of Christian education are so negative must not hide the further fact that people are being taught certain conceptions of the nature and will of God, and of human responsibility toward God. Even in these negative ways people are being taught something determinative as to God and as to man's responsibility to God.

On the other hand confrontation can be interpreted in such a way that exalting the divine initiative stimulates rather than discourages human initiative and the sense of human responsibility. This is precisely what is done in the Bible by means of the doctrine of the covenant and the doctrine of the *koinonia*. In the doctrine of the covenant both God's freedom *and* man's freedom, both God's responsibility to man *and* man's responsibility to God, are vividly set forth.

In the doctrine of the *koinonia* the Christian community by virtue of its own nature is the scene where God is constantly confronting man in the redemptive disclosure of himself. But the Christian community by virtue of its own nature is also the scene where men participate with one another in the encounter, and influence one another in the responses which they make to God.

This means, for example, that the fact of God's presence with man needs to be constantly interpreted to persons of all ages and stages of life so that they may perceive it. It means that the human response to revelation, while it is the direct response of an I to a Thou, is nevertheless open to the kind of guidance which one person may offer to another. And it means that the Christian community, in so far as it is indwelt by the Spirit, is a community where men participate in the redemptive and re-creative work of God in his forthgoing into human life.

The way thus is opened for a distinctive kind of education, appropriate to the Christian community and not possible in full scope and depth outside that community. It is distinctive first of all because when it views the human self it is concerned with the total self and its total well-being. It knows the existing self, living in anxiety, exposed to constant threat. But it knows that same self as made in the image of God, capable of abundant life which is everlasting.

It is distinctive because it is an education which bears witness to revelation. It testifies that God as Self discloses himself, moving in judgment and in redemption toward the human self, to the end that the existing self may become what it was created to be.

It is a distinctive education because of the nature of the society in which it is carried on. The Christian community, the scene of Christian education, is a worshiping community which is indwelt by the Spirit of God. Being indwelt by the Spirit, the relationships between the members are capable of becoming channels of the corrective, redemptive, and re-creative power of God. In such a society those who preach the Word of God and those who teach the Word of God are alike worthy of honor in that they are "laborers together with God." Yet in that co-laboring it is "God who gives the increase."

It is a distinctive education, again, in the center of its concern. It is concerned with the encounter between the Self-disclosing God and the responding human self. It is not concerned with God and his nature considered in abstraction from man and man's condition. It is not concerned with man and his needs considered apart from God. It is concerned with man in his need encountering God who confronts him in Self-giving.

Strictly speaking, then, this education is not God-centered, nor is it man-centered. It is bi-polar; that is, it is concerned with the *meeting* between God and the human creature, and with the tension which rises within the encounter, calling for human response to God and for divine response to man.

It is distinctive, still again, because of the nature of the results which take place within the encounter. It leads primarily not to knowledge *about* the self, but to self-knowledge. It leads primarily not to knowledge *about* God, but to knowledge *of* God. Put in Biblical terms it leads primarily not to *gnosis*, which is knowledge derived from philosophical or scientific inquiry, or may even be information derived from revelation. Rather it leads primarily to *epignosis*, which is the thorough knowledge that is de-

rived from the experience of man in his need responding positively to God in his Self-disclosure.

Put in terms of modern education, it leads primarily not to
information as such, but to the actual experience of the Person and
the events with which the information deals.

CHAPTER V

Predicament and Theme

WE HAVE NOW to inquire into the relation between the Bible and Christian education. This follows naturally after the inquiry into the relation between revelation and education. For just as the church is under the necessity of constantly examining its doctrine of the nature of revelation, so also it is under the necessity of constantly examining its doctrine of the nature of the Bible and of the relation between the Bible and Christian education.

WITNESSES TO REVELATION

In the preceding chapters it has been said that man in his anxiety and in his estrangement from himself, from his fellows, and from God is met by God who discloses himself in redemption; and that the scene where revelation takes place is the scene where fellowship exists. Revelation is not information about God; it is what happens in the meeting between God who gives himself and man who perceives and responds.

To this revelation there are two great witnesses: the church and the Bible. The church witnesses to revelation by the very fact of its continuing existence as a living community, the *Christian* church. It witnesses to revelation by being the scene of the continuing encounter between man and God. It witnesses to revelation by its worship of the God who has disclosed himself in the life, the passion, the death, and the resurrection of Jesus Christ. It witnesses by its proclamation of the gospel which affirms hope for man in the midst of despair. It witnesses by its teaching of the word of God, and by its care for the souls of men.

The Bible is a witness to revelation in that it contains the record of the original revelation by which the church was called into being and to which it owes its continuing existence. It is not the revelation itself, but points to it. It is the written record of the revelation to which the church as a living community continues to testify.

The Bible and the church stand in a close but strange relation to each other, in two respects. The first is that each is dependent upon the other. This dependence is so intimate that if they are separated, the Bible apart from the church becomes an object of scientific curiosity merely, or more likely a something to be forgotten; while the church separated from the Bible soon has little left to distinguish it from other human institutions.

This intimate relation between the Bible and the church had its origin in remote times. The church existed before the Bible. From a mass of religious writings the church selected the books which we now know as the Bible, and affirmed them to be canonical, that is, lawful for reading in the service of public worship. The purpose of the reading was to instruct the people. That instruction was itself a part of the service of worship. Thus the Bible is historically the bond of union by which worship and teaching are indissolubly wedded together into one service, both in Judaism and in Christianity.

But the Bible and the church bear a second relation to each other which is one of tension. Each is in tension with the other to such a degree that we could almost speak of an opposition between them. The Bible is in tension with the church because the revelation which the Bible records keeps the church always under the judgment of God, and stands ready always to demolish any prideful claims which the church or the ministry makes for itself.

The church is in tension with the Bible because the church knows it must face the Bible, and knows it must interpret the Bible to the people; and yet commonly contrives to censor it, or to soften it down, or evade it, or explain it away, or distort it, in interpreting it to the people.

The modern church stands where the ancient church stood, in that the Bible is the principal source from which the church's teaching is drawn. The modern church stands where the Reformation churches stood, in having had to rediscover this dependence and acknowledge it. But the modern church stands where the Reformation churches stood in this respect also: we believe that the Bible should be permitted to speak its own message to the people, but the people say they cannot understand it. We are therefore under the temptation to take away the very liberty which we profess we are offering. In taking it upon ourselves to proffer the help which the people ask, we expose them and ourselves as well to the very risk which we deplore; namely, creating a doctrine about the Bible which will then stand between the people and the Bible so that they no longer hear what it speaks.

This is the profound embarrassment of Protestantism. It is the road by which we may easily slip into a Protestant authoritarianism. This then takes the place of the Roman authoritarianism which we sought to escape. But if we constantly acknowledge this temptation and put the people on guard, we have at least declared that *we* are not the light, neither is the Bible itself the light, but both we and it witness to the Person who is light.

Introducing persons to the Bible, then, is one of the principal functions to be performed by the Christian community in its educational work. But because of the tension between the Bible and the church to which we have just alluded, and for other reasons as well, it has proved surprisingly difficult to establish sound principles for the use of the Bible in Christian education.

By way of seeking such principles we may ask what is the purpose of using the Bible in teaching; we may consider some of the principal problems that have to be met; we may ask in what sense the Bible is relevant to modern life; and we may ask whether it is possible to identify themes in the Bible which have permanent relevance to human need.

PURPOSE

We assume that the purpose of using the Bible in Christian education should be consistent with the nature of the Bible itself, and with the nature of the revelation to which it testifies. If revelation is God's disclosure of himself to man, and if the Bible contains the record of original revelation, what would be the central purpose of using the Bible in Christian education?

We suggest that it is to be sought in such terms as these. As already pointed out, the Bible faces us with the record of God's disclosure of himself through such media as physical nature, human nature, the events of history, and above all the life, death, and resurrection of Jesus Christ, the incarnate Word of God. The central purpose of using the Bible in Christian education is *to prepare the way for men to perceive God and respond to him in the present. We may call this the purpose of the continuing encounter.*

What the Bible describes is a continuing confrontation, continuing throughout human history, throughout the life of every religious community, and throughout the life of every individual person from birth to death. The Bible can awaken and foster man's continuing perception of this continuing divine confrontation, and can guide his continuing response to it.

Around that central purpose of the continuing encounter, and subsidiary to it, lie other contributory purposes. These purposes are legitimate and worthy so long as they are kept subordinate. Once they are allowed to become principal purposes they begin to make the Bible an end in itself instead of a means to the encounter with God. In that event they begin to convert the Bible into an object of worship and thus paralyze a truly spiritual use of it.

One such contributory purpose is to introduce the members of the Christian community in each generation to the revelatory events, the persons, the struggles, the defeats and the achievements which have gone into the making of our Jewish-Christian heritage. We are thinking here of that part of the story which is contained in the Bible, although the story runs its unbroken course from that day to this. When the Bible is used with this contributory purpose in view the religious community is helped to discharge its function of remembrance.

Such remembrance is not the indulgence of a homesick longing to return to the past. Neither is it a pious digging around in the rubbish of the past hoping to find useful religious antiques hidden here and there. It is literally being introduced to our heritage, coming to know the people to whom we owe so much, that sustains us.

It is an act of affirming that we participate in the life of a church that is undying, affirming that its history is our history, and that the way we bear ourselves in our encounter is a matter of concern to a great cloud of witnesses.

Another contributory purpose in using the Bible is that of learning to think and communicate in terms of Biblical symbols. The great questions and the great affirmations of the Jewish-Christian faith are couched in terms of symbols. These symbols constitute a remarkably rich vocabulary for communicating with one another in the Christian community regarding the ultimate issues of life and death. The Biblical records of encounter with God and the Biblical doctrines concerning God, man, sin, salvation, duty, and destiny are expressed in terms of this vocabulary.

Like any other form of speech, the meaning of these symbols is learned by use. Learning this vocabulary can easily become an end in itself in the Christian community, just because it is so important. To make a knowledge of the symbols an end in itself leads people to wander in a desert of preoccupation with such matters as dispensations, or theological, liturgical, and ecclesiastical minutiae. In this event the Bible ceases to be a living voice, and becomes a thing to be put under the microscope.

But when knowledge of the symbols is kept contributory to the greater purpose of preparing the way for the encounter which they symbolize, the symbols introduce us to the language common to all who journey deeply into the Bible. They are the speech in which we may learn how to ask the major questions of human existence. They are the speech in which Heaven has spoken to earth as touching these matters of such high import.

Still another contributory purpose in using the Bible is that of inquiring whether the Bible throws any light upon the place where we stand at the present moment of existence. This is the search for the relevance of revelation. It expresses the concern to know whether the Bible has anything to say on behalf of God concerning the complex issues of living in the present world. The term long used to denote this purpose is "searching the Scriptures."

As with other contributory purposes, so here; searching the Scriptures can degenerate. It can, for example, become a matter of

trying to settle intricate ethical problems by appealing to particular
Biblical passages, much as one would cite a statute in a code of law.
This is legalism, which in this case makes the Bible the master of
men.

Searching the Scriptures can become mere practicalism. Here
the Bible is called upon somewhat like an oracle, in the hope that it
will answer the specific questions which we are ready to ask. But
it is given no opportunity to speak its greatest utterances because
we have no "felt need" for them. This almost exactly reverses legalism, and makes man the master of the Bible. It has proved to be one
of the most effective of all ways of putting the Bible under lock and
key.

But even though the search for relevance can take distorted
forms, the search itself must go on in each generation. It means
taking living questions to the Bible, hoping to hear living answers.
The nature of the search for relevance changes with the passing of
time. Later in this chapter we shall point to one of the forms which
it is now taking, with important consequences for Christian education.

If the central purpose in using the Bible is to prepare the way
for the continuing encounter, the Christian community is the scene
above all others where the Bible can be used in education in a way
which is wholly consistent with the nature of the Bible itself and
with the nature of the revelation to which it points. For in the
Christian community as a *worshiping* community the encounter
with God, to which the Bible testifies, goes on constantly in the
present. In this setting perception can be quickened, and positive
responses to God can arise; the more readily so because of the interaction between persons which goes on in the Christian community.

On the negative side this means that teaching the Bible in a
scene outside the Christian community, or teaching it anywhere in
separation from worship, is an undertaking attended by heavy
handicaps. When the Bible is lifted out of its relation to the worshipful encounter, it easily becomes a lifeless thing. It cannot speak
because the ear is not open to hear what it has to say, and the questions which we put to the Bible outside the worshipful encounter
are questions to which the Bible is quite indifferent.

If the central purpose in using the Bible is to prepare the way for personal encounter within the context of the worshiping community, we can be set free from another purpose which has dogged the use of the Bible like an evil genius. This is using the Bible as a means whereby we try to manipulate the conduct of the members of the Christian community. It involves picking materials from the Bible and using them as means for putting pressure on the young to follow our notions of Christian conduct. This is the moralistic use of the Bible. It has perhaps done more than any other one thing to cause the young to regard religious teaching with suspicion and put up their guard against it.

But if the central purpose is personal encounter, the way is left open for developing types of teaching which are characterized by becoming involved in the Bible, in contrast with being put under pressure from the Bible. Such teaching will help persons, both young and old, to encounter the Bible itself and what it contains. It will help them to stand within the Bible, participating in what is there described. It lets it happen that the God who spoke then can be heard now. It is teaching which understands the question asked in the spiritual: "Were you there when they crucified my Lord?"

Furthermore, if the central purpose is to prepare the way for personal encounter we shall be able to deal in a straightforward manner with some of the problems that have arisen in connection with instruction in the content of the Bible. In recent years much has been said, and well said, as to the dangers of an education which is merely transmission or merely indoctrination. As a result of this wholesome warning, however, many who bear a responsibility for education have become afraid to speak frankly of instruction, much less to engage in it openly. They have felt it necessary to indulge in all sorts of methodological devices so as to skirt around frankly giving instruction.

But if the central purpose in using the Bible is that of preparing the way for perceiving and responding to the God who discloses himself through physical nature, through human nature, through the events of history, and through the life, death, and resurrection of Jesus Christ—if this is the central purpose it is not only permissible, it is necessary to include instruction in Biblical content as part of the curriculum. The Bible is, so to speak, the mother tongue of the Christian community, and we cannot talk of the deepest concerns of the human soul in Christian terms without knowing this language.

It is easy, moreover, to underestimate the readiness of the young for a certain amount of direct instruction in matters of religion. In the natural course of living, scores of questions are raised in their minds, making them want information as to fact. This seems to be true whether one lives in a homogeneous community such as a village, or in the pluralistic culture of a great city. The point is that the young are exposed to a question-raising world. And endless stories are told nowadays of children who are discontented in the church school because they are "getting nothing."

This does not mean that the curriculum materials of Christian education should consist of nothing but the Bible. It does mean that some acquaintance with what is in the Bible is necessary if one is to hear what is being said to us there in preparation for our own encounter. The sincere effort to stand within this book and participate in the profound struggles there depicted has the effect of causing the Bible to "come alive." It is this coming alive which is needed as a result of teaching the Bible within the Christian community, if the Bible is to help prepare the way for personal encounter between the man of today and the God of whom the Bible speaks.

PROBLEMS

While it is assumed that the nature of the Bible should govern our purpose in using it, we have to recognize that the nature of the Bible also creates difficulties which tend to stand in the way of achieving that purpose.

For one thing the Bible is a very human book. This is a fact in which the Christian community can take deep satisfaction, since it keeps so much of the Bible so close to the human situation as we know it. Nevertheless it raises problems which are the more pressing in proportion as one insists that the Bible is a record of divine revelation.

For when it is urged that the Bible contains the record of

original revelation, it has to be recognized at once that the divine Self-disclosure was revelation to *human selves*. In order to be revelation at all, it had to be perceived *by men*. Both the original perception of revelation and the report of that perception are inevitably conditioned by human psychological processes. They are colored by the personal history of the men to whom the revelation came, and by the cultural history not of Israel only but of much of the ancient world.

The Bible is a human book in another sense also. After being written its books were subject to the vicissitudes of human history. Its text had to be transmitted through copying until printing was invented. Parts of the text have been corrupted in transmission, so that at many points we cannot be certain what the correct text is. And the canon, or list of books included in the Bible, was determined by men and councils of men. Even today the term "the Bible" does not mean the same to all Christians; for Roman Catholics include in it the books of the Apocrypha, while Protestants do not.

If we are not to fall into obscurantism as regards the human element in the Bible, we need to use the Bible with due regard for all the light that can be thrown upon it from historical, literary, or textual criticism; or from research in archaeology, anthropology, and psychology. Yet the findings in all these fields of study are themselves subject to error. In trying to escape from the tyranny of an authoritarian use of the Bible, it is easy to fall into the equally authoritarian use of "the latest results of scientific study," which are then allowed to dictate what we may or may not do with the Bible.

Thus we are put in a dilemma. Since the findings on many important points are not all in, or since we suppose the people are not yet ready to absorb the shock of becoming acquainted with facts which every scholarly student knows, we may withhold knowledge of scholarly work which affects the Bible. But in that event we put the Bible in a false light, we expose those whom we teach to the later conclusion that their teachers were either ignorant or deceitful; and we have to make peace with ourselves for having entered into a conspiracy for the suppression of knowledge.

But if we present our knowledge of the human element in the Bible, we run into risks of a contrasted kind. For example, what we say about the Bible may be quite as seriously in error as is the point of view we are seeking to counteract. Or we may overwhelm the revelation of God by a not very inspiring revelation of ourselves, parading our "knowledge." Or being very busy destroying idols that need to be destroyed, we may come to realize rather late in the day that we have put nothing positive in their place.

A kindred difficulty in using the Bible arises from the fact that it is a book from an ancient day. The civilizations which march across its pages so hauntingly long ago fell into decay, or disappeared wholly from the face of the earth. Its central country, Palestine, is foreign to most of the people who hear or read the Bible. Many of the objects which hold a crucial place in the narratives and in the symbolism, and many of the customs which give a story its point, are wholly unfamiliar to persons living in the modern Western world.

This places us under two temptations. One is the temptation of losing our way among details concerning geography, politics, customs, modern explorations and excavations, and the like. The other is the temptation to modernize the scenes, the problems, and the persons of the Bible. Thus in the effort to show that the Bible is interesting, one easily slips into preoccupation with matters of less and less importance as far as encounter is concerned; while in the effort to show that the Bible is relevant, one slips with equal ease into presenting as Biblical what is not in the Bible at all.

Another difficulty, not unrelated to the two just mentioned, arises from the fact that the Bible is written in ancient languages which must be translated into modern speech. But in translating it is almost impossible to reproduce the exact shades of meaning expressed in the original. This requires a delicate balance between fidelity to the exact language of an ancient writer, and sensitivity to the meaning of words in the speech of a modern hearer or reader of the Bible.

The appearance of so many modern translations of the Bible is evidence of present concern in the Christian community over this phase of the problem of communication. The rather temperate arguments for the merits of this or that translation suggest that it is impossible for any one translation to meet all the needs felt in this area. The rather explosive arguments that have arisen over changing the English translation of a single Hebrew or Greek word suggest the extreme difficulty of hearing what the Bible is actually saying, once one has made up his mind that he knows. And the distress of many persons in the English-speaking world when they learn that the King James Version is not the direct output of the men who wrote the Bible suggests how much groundwork needs to be done in every generation before the nature of the Bible itself can be understood. Each of these constitutes an important problem in the use of the Bible.

Again, much of the Bible is inherently difficult to understand, so much so as to raise serious problems when it comes to using these portions in teaching. Many allusions are obscure, as in the prophets. Some especially important lines of argument are so involved as to be very difficult to follow, as in certain passages in Paul's writings, and in the epistle to the Hebrews. Some passages are offensive to modern sensibilities, as are some psychological and physiological terms which occur very frequently.

Some of the thought forms employed in the Bible are alien to the Western mind. This is especially the case with the apocalyptic and eschatological passages in the prophets, in the Gospels, in the epistles, and in the book of Revelation. And many of the symbols by which Biblical meanings are communicated are by no means easy to grasp. For such reasons it is little wonder that the portions of the Bible which seem easy to understand should be as prominent as they are in the use of the Bible, while parts that are more difficult to understand may be seriously neglected. Yet it is in this latter category that many of the most profound Biblical doctrines regarding God's revelation of himself are to be found.

Still again, the fact that the Bible contains two "testaments" raises a group of problems which have to be met in using the Bible in the Christian community. The principal question, of course, is how the Christian teacher shall deal with the Old Testament in general, and with its systems of ethics in particular. The Old Testament presents the constant demand for obedience to the specific requirements of the Mosaic law, the Torah. This law is presented in the Old Testament as the law of God. Blessing of every kind is promised to those who keep it, while suffering and calamity are commonly interpreted as visitations of God upon those who have not met the obligations of the law.

Now if the Christian teacher proposes to let the Bible speak for itself with a minimum of distortion, and if he presents the Old Testament in this manner, he is still moving within the realm of Judaism. He is teaching within the Christian community, but *what* he is teaching is the Jewish faith and the Jewish way of life. What is of crucial importance is that he lives within the Christian community, but teaches the Jewish system of ethics.

This is exactly what has happened many times in the history of the Christian church. Whenever it does happen it represents a regression from Christianity to Judaism. It means superimposing the Jewish conception of ethics onto the Christian community which by its own nature has been set free from the Jewish conception of ethics. Judaism sought wholeness for the self by obedience to the law, while Christianity sought it by faith in a Person. The New Testament tells the story of the struggle between these two great systems, and their eventual separation from each other.

If then the Christian teacher proposes to let the Old Testament speak for itself in all its richness, but if at the same time he proposes to interpret the Old Testament in the light of the New Testament, he must find the principle by which he will relate them. If he is convinced that revelation is God's disclosure of himself to man, and if he is convinced that this Self-disclosure came to its culmination in the incarnation, the passion, and the resurrection of Jesus Christ, these convictions will offer him the basis for the principle by which he can relate the two Testaments to each other.

We shall illustrate the use of such a principle when we come to speak of the themes of the Bible. But more important than that, it is to be remembered that the New Testament itself abundantly illustrates the way in which those who believed in Jesus as the Christ reoriented themselves to the Old Testament.

Once more, we have the problem of relevance. We have already referred to the search for relevance as being one of the contributary purposes in using the Bible. It still remains to ask, What is the principle of relevance?

Relevance in Biblical material has been sought in many ways. At the risk of seriously oversimplifying we may say that the search for relevance tends to move in one or the other of two principal directions: toward external relevance or toward internal relevance. By the search for external relevance we mean that the portions of the Bible which are considered to be the most significant for human life are those that prescribe how life should be lived. This is the part or element in the Bible that stresses duty, obligation, law, and obedience to law.

By the search for internal relevance we mean that the portions of the Bible which are considered to be the most significant for human life are those that are concerned with the situation that exists within man. It lifts into prominence those elements in the Bible that are concerned with disaster and with triumph in the inward man. It is a search for that aspect of the record of revelation most relevant to what we earlier called the existing self. It seeks the points at which revelation bears directly upon the situation of the existing human self.

Both these kinds of relevance can, of course, be found in the Bible. And they are not mutually exclusive in any complete way. But the New Testament emphasis on faith as contrasted with obedience to law plainly casts the weight of the New Testament on the side of relationship as contrasted with external performance. Salvation conceived as wholeness of self in relationship tends to drive out salvation conceived as status earned by living up to a prescribed pattern.

Considerations of this kind lead us to seek the principle of relevance primarily in terms of internal relevance. This in turn underlies the conception of revelation as relevant to human predicament, a conception now to be further examined.

RELEVANCE

It is desirable now to look still further into the question of the relevance of the Bible, especially what we have just referred to as internal relevance. The Bible, we have been saying, is a witness to revelation in that it contains the record of original revelation. When we ask what the relevance of the Bible is, we are really asking what the relevance of revelation is.

We have already approached the question of the nature of revelation from two points of departure. One is the situation of the human creature, made in the image of God and yet existing in a state of anxiety and often of estrangement. The other is the Self-giving of God, who discloses himself to man in his existing situation with corrective, redemptive and re-creative power. *The relevance of revelation lies in the fact that the disclosure fits the need. It is Self meeting self. It is the disclosure of that profound Selfhood in God which eventually is the deepest mystery of our universe. But it is not a disclosure into a vacuum. It is a disclosure from God which matches the need in the existing self of man, and can call forth the capacities of that self.*

On grounds such as these we establish what may be called the principle of correspondence between divine revelation and human need.[1] This principle points to a personal mutuality which is most simply indicated by such terms as "call" and "answer." The call is either from God to man, or from man to God. And so with the answer; it is either from God to man or from man to God. The answer is in response to the call, and fits the call as the glove fits the hand.

If this is true of revelation it should also be true of the Bible which is the record of revelation. The Bible would then be perceived as a document which is living because it contains the record of living answers to living questions. The questions are living questions because they arise generation after generation. The answers are living answers because they are relevant generation after generation. They pertain to something that is of vital import. They deal with issues of life and death. The Bible can be used as a living book because it testifies to the correspondence between man's persisting need and God's revelation of himself.

In using the Bible in the church it becomes necessary to work out the details of the Biblical witness to the correspondence between human need and divine revelation. It is possible in principle for this to be done from either side of the relation, that is, beginning either with human need or with divine revelation. But wherever we begin, the mutuality is the same. If we begin with human need as a starting point in teaching and move toward the Bible, the Bible witnesses to a Self-disclosure of God which is relevant to human need. If we start with the record of revelation, the revelation is relevant to man in need.

We may now consider each of these as a point of departure from which to arrive at the mutuality of the encounter between man and God: beginning with human need, and beginning with the Biblical record of revelation.

PREDICAMENT

It is possible to start from human need and then move toward the Bible, searching for those parts of the Bible which are relevant. This is the spontaneous way in which the Bible is used by those who know it well enough to move about in it with a sense of familiarity.

If this is the basis for planned teaching, it is necessary to define what is meant by "need," and to secure an analysis of existing need. The task of defining human need is more basic than the task of analyzing existing needs, because the definition determines what is to be analyzed. Definition of the nature of human need is a task for philosophical or theological thought; the analysis of need is a task for scientific method. If this distinction is observed, scientific method can be the servant of inquiry. If the distinction is obliterated scientism becomes our master, telling us what we shall think.

When the nature and the extent of human need have been determined as far as is possible for purposes of this kind, experiences can be planned and materials selected which are relevant to the need. Biblical materials can of course be included within the total of the materials used.

In a somewhat similar manner it is possible to start from a "felt problem" and move toward the Bible in search of relevant parts of the record. The concept of the problem has been much used in modern religious teaching. It is often employed as the starting point in guiding the experience of groups. Thus a group may be led to recognize the existence of a problem, to analyze it, to formulate

hypothetical solutions, to search for relevant data, and to put one
or more of the hypothetical solutions to the test of experience. In
this method of teaching, the search for data frequently means that a
group goes to the Bible in quest of records of relevant previous experience.[2]

The approach to the Bible which starts from the definition and
analysis of human need, and that which starts from a felt problem,
give a sense of immediacy to the Bible. Either of these is literally the
pursuit of knowledge. Under good teaching it becomes an exciting
affair. Whoever achieves such a result in teaching the Bible certainly has much to his credit.

But the constant use of these approaches, unrelieved by any
others, tends toward a practicalism in the use of the Bible which
may keep the sense of need at a shallow level, blur the perception
of the more profound internal relevance of the Bible, and defeat the
central purpose of the continuing encounter. One begins then to
refer to the Bible as a handbook, or a sourcebook. This is not far
removed from making the Bible a religious encyclopedia, or even a
religious almanac to be consulted in moments of uncertainty. These
approaches render honor to relevance, but commonly they fail to
get at an element of depth in human need which is unmistakably
present in the record of revelation.

Partly for reasons of this kind it is becoming common now to
use the term "predicament" in preference to such terms as "need"
and "problem" when the more profound aspects of the human
situation are under view, as they are when one speaks of anxiety,
estrangement, helplessness, and the like. We shall use the term "predicament" to refer to some persisting human concern, which tends
to recur generation after generation, century after century. *The
sense of predicament arises out of the profound anxiety which we
carry as human creatures in an existence where every form of security tends to be threatened sooner or later.*

Predicament, as we have indicated, is deeper than what is
usually meant by such terms as "need" and "problem." These latter
terms tend to be more specific than "predicament." The more specific needs and problems take their particular shape for individual
selves because the deep underlying anxiety has been stirred up by

threats to the existing self. To deal with the particular needs and problems as specifics without recognizing their deeper rootage in the underlying anxiety is to run the risk of dealing with symptoms while ignoring the more profound anxiety. If the specific needs and problems are taken care of without getting at their rootage, the anxiety will probably express itself promptly in some new form.

The sense of predicament takes on various forms in the course of human history. But predicament has certain characteristics which seem to pervade its various forms. For example, a sense of predicament arises when we face some profound issue in personal or social life and begin to recognize that the solution of particular problems, one by one, is getting us nowhere, or is even getting us in deeper. This is the beginning of hopelessness and despair. And while the despair may be the prelude to the search for a solution at a more profound level, it is by no means certain that this will be so. Hence predicament may sap the will to live.

When we seek the solution at a more profound level, the predicament may take on the form of a still deeper dilemma. In this event the choice between the newly seen alternatives is extremely difficult, because no one alternative seems capable of relieving the profound anxiety. If we choose either horn of one of these deeper dilemmas where ambiguity still persists, we may become very aggressive in defending the solution we have chosen, being defensive and aggressive about it just because we are fundamentally insecure in the choice which we have made. Many attempts at the religious solution of human predicament are arrested at this level.

A predicament when seen in its deeper meanings sometimes arouses the strong feeling that *no* solution is possible at all. The road seems completely blocked. This results in a sense of profound frustration, and tempts us either to give up completely, or to escape in some manner such as going back to a more superficial solution which may be praised as "the good old way."

And predicament has this disturbing quality about it, that when a profound predicament is met by a profound solution, another and perhaps even more difficult predicament begins to appear on the horizon. Thus the dimensions of human anxiety begin to be more apparent in proportion as we penetrate the more deeply beneath human "problems" and into the nature of the underlying human predicament.

In using the Bible it is possible to start with the Bible and move toward human need. It has just been observed that when we start from human need and move toward the Bible, it is necessary to define the nature of human need and to analyze its existing forms. The reverse of this is also true. If we start with the Bible and move toward human need, it is necessary to define the nature of the Bible, and to analyze what it contains. We have already discussed the nature of the Bible as containing a record of revelation, thus witnessing to revelation.

We have next to consider, then, how the material that is in the Bible is to be analyzed for the purpose of using it in the Christian community. We assume now that the central purpose in using it is the purpose of preparing the way for the continuing encounter. We assume that there are legitimate secondary purposes in using it, such as discharging the function of remembrance, and gaining an acquaintance with the symbols of communication within the Christian community. And we assume that what we are seeking in any analysis of the Bible for purposes of this kind is that aspect of revelation which is relevant to human need, especially to human predicament, which is the more profound form of human need.

We propose that the analysis of the Bible and the selection of materials from it for the purpose of teaching in the Christian community can be made in terms of themes that are found in the Bible. The concept "theme" refers to some aspect of God's Self-disclosure to man which persists more or less prominently throughout the Bible.

Themes have to be selected with great attentiveness to what is in the Bible itself, so that they may be themes which spring out of the Bible and are not foisted upon it. Since the doctrine of revelation changes in the church with the passing of time, it is to be expected that if the principle of themes is sound the perception of the themes that are in the Bible will change also.

We have no thought of offering a final list of themes, but it seems desirable to illustrate the method and some of its results. Accordingly we propose this statement: *Revelation is God's disclosure of himself in creation, in lordship, in vocation, in judgment, in re-demption, in re-creation, in providence, and in the life of faith; the Bible contains these themes, and each of them is in correspondence with some profound human predicament.*

Certain general statements need to be made regarding principles which underlie the concept of themes. To begin with, it is well to distinguish between the history which is in the Bible, and the themes of the Bible. The history deals with particular events which are concrete and specific. Specific events recorded in the Bible are presented to us as a medium through which revelation may be perceived. What a particular revelatory event utters is "a word from the Lord" to those who are able to perceive it.

But when a long series of revelatory events speaks to one persisting human predicament, what is uttered in the long series of revelatory events becomes a theme. Something which hangs together is being said in many ways to many men through centuries of time. The events of Biblical history which have been perceived as revelatory events thus become the concrete ground into which continuing revelation has come, and in which the continuing perception of revelation has arisen in response.

This means that the events which the Bible presents to us are the indispensable stuff out of which the themes are built. This is the reason why we have insisted that while the central purpose of using the Bible is that of the continuing encounter, a contributory but inescapable purpose is that of introducing the members of the Christian community to the persons and the events that have been media of revelation. The themes of revelation transcend specific persons and events, and transcend all particular times and places; yet they are always rooted in specific persons and events.

Again: it will be understood from what has been previously said that a theme tends to appear throughout the Bible. We are not required, however, to find a given theme in every book of the Bible, nor are we required to find all the themes in each book of the Bible. It is enough if we understand that they pervade the Bible. They are, so to speak, the notes on which the great symphony of redemption is constructed, and they keep on appearing and reappearing.

The themes are not sharply separated from one another, nor are they mutually exclusive of one another. On the contrary, they are deeply intertwined throughout the Bible. But each if them does lend itself to consideration as a distinctive strand in the greater whole.

Each of the themes comes to culmination in the life, death, and resurrection of Jesus Christ. In him revelatory selfhood and revelatory revelation are oriented. Eventually this means that the relevance of Jesus Christ to every predicament of human life is, or may be, perceived.

When a theme is viewed in its long sweep throughout the Bible, it will ordinarily be found to contain a tension within itself. All the parts of a theme are not saying the same thing. Two or more contrasted or even opposing expressions of a theme are frequent. The most notable of these tensions is that between the theme as expressed in the Old Testament, and the same theme as expressed in the New Testament. But there may also be a tension between the differing ways in which a particular theme is expressed in different parts of the Old Testament. Similarly there may be a tension between the differing ways in which a particular theme is expressed within different parts of the New Testament.

We are under no compulsion to bring all the expressions of a given theme into complete uniformity. The use of themes makes it possible to present specific parts of the Bible so that they will stand forth in their own right, in full force, without being tampered with to make them say something else. But the use of themes also makes it possible to present these parts in such a way that they will not be disparate fragments, but will be seen as parts in a large purposeful movement of continuing Self-disclosure.

Each theme is relevant to a profound human predicament. This is the nature of the ultimate relevance of the themes. They have to do with the profoundest needs of men, those persisting predicaments which are rooted in the normal anxiety of human existence. Each theme is as it were the record of a very long dialogue, now of call and reply, now of question and answer, between God and man as deep calls unto deep.

If the principle of predicament and theme is soundly conceived, the themes themselves can become the basis for the selection of Biblical materials to be used in the curriculum of Christian education. They are the more suitable for this purpose if stated so as to bring out the dynamic interaction between God as Self and man as a self, to which the Biblical record of revelation so constantly testifies.

CORRESPONDENCE

To illustrate the principle of correspondence still further, we suggest a tentative schematization. Each of the eight themes mentioned will be defined, and a statement will be proposed as to the predicament toward which it points. It must be borne in mind that any such statements as these are highly abstract in form, and tentative as to content. The themes of the Bible and the predicaments of man come to life only as they are filled in with the concrete materials of the Bible and the shape of man's anxiety in the midst of existence.

Creation. God's disclosure of himself in creation is his giving of himself in continuing creativity, and presenting the results of that creativity to man for his perception, use, and enjoyment. Our universe, the world and all it contains, man with his potentiality, and any other living creatures who may exist anywhere in the universe, are perceived in the Bible as owing their origin and their continuance to the creative power of God.

The theme of creation is set over against the predicament of man's misapprehension of himself, his world, and God; and of his own relation to his world and God. The redemptive element in the theme of creation derives from the fact that it calls man away from his misapprehension of the nature of the world, and calls him toward a perception of the true nature of the world and man, and their relation to God.

Lordship. God's disclosure of himself in lordship is his confronting men as the sovereign of all that has been, and of all that is, in this age and in that which is to come. In the Biblical view nothing is excluded from this sovereignty, for he who created is Lord over all that he has made.

The theme of lordship is pointed toward the predicament of man's freedom. As a created being he is under the lordship of God. But as man he is given the freedom to choose; and this freedom, high-water mark of his humanity, threatens always to be his undoing. This holds true in many respects, but here attention can be restricted to the necessity of constantly choosing between competing claims upon a man's supreme loyalty and devotion. Biblically this necessity is constantly being pointed up by facing us with some form of the demand, "Choose ye this day whom ye will serve."

Vocation. God's disclosure of himself in vocation is his calling on man to enter a relationship with him in which his lordship is recognized. In general, vocation is the call to enter the covenant relationship, and to discharge the obligations of that relationship, within the religious society. This call is a call to all men to devote all of life to the sovereignty of God. In general, then, vocation is social because it is a call into the religious society, universal because it is a call to all men, and total because it is a call upon the individual self in its totality. In particular, vocation is the call to discharge some specific function or mission.

The predicament toward which the theme of vocation is pointed is the predicament of the demonic element in human society. Man as a social creature must live a social existence, and cannot live in isolation from his fellows. This human society which he must have is good in myriad ways. The more we know of its beneficent functions in producing and sustaining man's selfhood, the more we do obeisance to the constructive power which operates through human society.

Nevertheless there is an element in human society so hostile to human values and so destructive of human selfhood that we can only call it demonic. Man works against himself as well as for himself, whether we state the case in individual or in social terms. And as long as a society undertakes to function without any corrective from beyond itself, it is subject to its own demonic forces as well as to its own beneficent forces. What is building itself up is also tearing itself down. When the destructive forces are in the ascendancy, society is sick and ever growing sicker.

Judgment. God's disclosure of himself in judgment is his rejection of whatever in man or in the works of man is contaminated by sin. It is God in the wholeness of his Selfhood confronting man in the splitness of his human selfhood and in his rebellion against the lordship of God. It is the holiness of God confronting the sinfulness of man. As with vocation, so with judgment: it is both individual and social. In Biblical terms God's judgment reveals his own holiness, his righteousness, his glory, and his wrath.

The theme of judgment is pointed toward the predicament of man's estrangement from God, and increases the gravity of that predicament. There is an estrangement from God which desires no reconciliation. But this does not mean that only those outside the covenant are under judgment. Always those who are within the covenant and inside the religious society are under judgment. Thus the most profound personal estrangement from God may exist within the religious community in the case of persons who sought to make their peace with God only to feel themselves under greater condemnation as they are confronted by God in his holiness, righteousness, and glory.

Redemption. God's disclosure of himself in redemption is his moving toward the human creature, to the end that estrangement may be overcome in reconciliation. Biblically understood, to redeem a person or even an object is to restore it to its rightful place in a relationship in which it belongs, but from which it has been alienated.[3] Thus the concept of redemption is peculiarly apt in reference to the restoring of a broken relationship between man and God.

The theme of redemption is pointed toward the predicament of man's estrangement from God, just as the theme of judgment is. There is no sharp line of distinction between estrangement from God, estrangement from one's fellows, and estrangement from oneself. But in the theme of redemption the center of concern is estrangement from God. In the theme of redemption, as in the theme of judgment, man has sinned and come short of the glory of God. But whereas in judgment God rejects, in redemption he moves toward the human self to seek him, to find him, to heal him of his hurt, and to bring him home. In redemption is revealed the love of God, his *agape*.

Re-creation. God's disclosure of himself in re-creation is his forth-going, not only to create the world and man, but also to re-create that which has been marred by the exercise of man's freedom. Redemption and re-creation are so intimately related that separating them incurs the risk of making both of them seem artificial. The same is true of the relation between creation and re-creation. But the theme of re-creation stresses God's activity of renewing, and the newness which results within man and his world.

The theme of re-creation is pointed toward the predicament of man's estrangement from himself. Any form of splitness within the self means that a man is estranged from himself. And there is a splitness in the self so deep that the self is divided against itself in one of the principal roots of its being, the will. The self, in schism within itself and unable to attain full selfhood, cannot make itself whole because it cannot initiate the decisive movement. It must have help from without; this is redemption. And it must become a new self within; this is re-creation.

Providence. God's disclosure of himself in providence is the exercise of his sovereign will through all the vicissitudes of existence in such a way that his love ultimately overcomes evil. As a consequence, ultimate meaning can be perceived in the existence of man and the universe, and this meaning is morally good, even as God himself is good.

The theme of providence is pointed toward the predicament of undiscerned meaning, that is, the predicament of man who is in the midst of existence, capable of discerning meaning in existence and longing to find meaning in it, and yet can discern no meaning in what is happening within him or within those he loves, no meaning in what is happening to himself or to them, no meaning in what is taking place in the world.

Such a predicament arises out of the perennial question, "Does personal life, does the history of mankind, does the universe itself have any meaning?" To fail to ask this question is to fail to be fully human. But to ask it is to face bafflement. For if we reply that these things have no meaning beyond the operations of blind chance, the mind still will not rest but keeps on asking, "What does it mean that there is no meaning in anything?" But if we reply that there is meaning, ultimate meaning at that, then we must not only affirm the meaning which we perceive; we must also stand before the mystery of good and evil.

The life of faith. God's disclosure of himself in the life of faith is his imparting of himself in daily life to those who give themselves to him. The life of faith thus is a mutual self-giving between God and man. As it gains in depth it becomes an interpenetration of selves as between the divine Self and the human self, but never to the obscuring of the selfhood of either. Biblically this interpenetration is expressed by saying that either Christ or the Spirit is in the believer, and by also saying that the believer is in Christ or in the Spirit.

The life of faith is based on two great affirmations. One is that man may live his daily life in fellowship with God. This is the affirmation of fellowship. The other is that a man in fellowship with God has the responsibility of determining his own conduct in the light of that fellowship. This is the affirmation of freedom. The one is fellowship with God, the other is freedom under God. Both have to do with the conduct of the daily life. One of the most apt of the many Biblical terms for the life of faith is "the walk with God."

The theme of the life of faith is pointed toward the predicament of the uncharted way. The "uncharted way" is only the obvious lot of every man, who is inexorably borne onward into the future but finds his own anxiety aroused by the unknowable elements in that future, and by his own freedom. In the life of faith, human freedom *as predicament* is transformed into freedom *as inalienable gift* in the fellowship between God and men.

ANXIETY AND GOSPEL

The themes taken as a whole correspond to the most profound predicament of all, the predicament of normal anxiety.[4] It is more important to see this basic correspondence between man's predica-

ment and God's revelation than it is to state a precise correspondence between particular forms of predicament and particular
themes of revelation. For the basic principle of correspondence
means that whatever the particular shape of the circumstances that
threaten him, man is not forsaken in the dangers that surround him.

The structure of the Bible itself is witness to the principle of
correspondence. When we examine the Bible as a whole, putting
particular books and groups of books against the times in which
they were written, the results become very impressive. Much that
we count richest in the record of revelation is set over against times
of profound anxiety.

For example, in the Old Testament the prophets of the eighth
and seventh centuries before Christ spoke or wrote in a time when
the nation was collapsing and moving on toward catastrophe. Much
of the rest of the Old Testament was either written or assembled
into its present form during a period marked by national humilia-
tion, by exile in strange lands, and by religious reconstruction
which had to be carried out under conditions of foreign political
domination.

The New Testament also was written against a background of
peril and anxiety. Of its twenty-seven books, some twenty probably were written between about A.D. 50 and 110. That period witnessed the reign of Nero and his persecutions. It saw the siege and
fall of Jerusalem with the destruction of the temple and the col-
lapse of the system of sacrificial worship. In those years came the
separation of Christianity from its matrix in Judaism, and the
Roman demand to worship the "genius" of the emperor or suffer
the consequences. All these have left deep traces in the books of
the New Testament.

In the Biblical understanding of life it is perceived that man's
anxiety arises in the face of peril which is both real and profound.
But it is perceived also that God's love is stronger than man's
anxiety, and can overcome it. Wherever this is genuinely believed,
it is the ground of a tremendous affirmation both of God and of
human life. Such an affirmation is good news, gospel.

The Christian life is a mixture of believing this and of doubting it. But human anxiety and the gospel of God are the two great counterparts in the Bible. The depth of each, their meeting in one Man, and the triumph of the love of God over the anxiety of man, are uttered for all time in the life, passion, death, and resurrection of Jesus Christ.

CHAPTER VI

Communication Through Symbols

UNTIL NOW WE have been speaking chiefly of human predicament, divine revelation, and man's encounter with God. These are central in the life of the Christian community. We have now to ask, How do we communicate with one another regarding such concerns as these?

This question and its answer are, of course, basic in any understanding of Christian education. The question itself follows naturally after we have inquired as to the nature of revelation and its content. The sequence of major questions is somewhat as follows: How has God communicated with man? How then do we for our part communicate with one another regarding the encounter with God in such a manner as to prepare the way for, and participate in, the continuing encounter within the Christian community?

COMMUNICATION

The subject of communication has taken on fresh significance in modern times, and is being investigated from many points of view. In the midst of this awakening concern we are faced by a rather strange paradox.

One aspect of the paradox can be stated in the truism that we live in an age of communication. The reasons which justify calling this an age of communication are familiar enough. Through such media as newspapers, magazines, and books the printed word is spread. Through radio and television the audible and visible word is disseminated. These and many other forms of communication carry entertainment, information, education, and propaganda to great masses of human beings. There is every reason to call this an age of communication.

The other side of the paradox is that in an age of communication great numbers of people are in danger of perishing for want of communication. This dangerous want of communication grows out of the separateness of many human beings from their kind, with the result that they live in isolation, loneliness, and emptiness. Not the least of the perils of this separateness exists in the very places where the greatest numbers of people are herded together, as in the cities.

In many cases the need to communicate is so great that persons will go under if the need is not met. The strength of the desire to secure it is indicated by the demand for the services of psychiatrists, analysts, clinical psychologists, and counselors of many kinds. Beyond these professionally competent persons lies a hinterland of others whose competence is dubious, but to whom distressed persons turn nevertheless for help.

When we say that this is an age of communication but that many persons are in danger of perishing for want of communication, it is apparent that "communication" has at least two quite different meanings. The first of these we may call one-way communication, because what is being communicated flows all in one direction. It is communication by pressure; for it is an effort to do something to people, such as to get them to buy, or to persuade them to do this or to believe that. Communication by pressure is aptly called "putting it across."

The most disturbing feature about one-way communication is that the more it increases in the world, the greater is our need to resist it. We have to armor ourselves against it; for if we do not do so, we lose our own integrity and become robots to be pulled and hauled from outside ourselves. But the more we close ourselves against it, the less is our separateness overcome. As the world becomes more and more filled with people trying to get inside our minds and emotions, the isolation of individuals, so far from being penetrated healingly, may only increase.

By contrast with one-way communication there is what we may call two-way communication. In this, communication flows in both directions, back and forth between two or more persons. It has mutuality in it, for each gives forth something of himself. It is communication by participation; for each takes part in the life of the other, especially in the interior life of the other; and this he does by the ready willingness of the other and not by pressure upon him.

In two-way communication at its best no person is an object to another person. No person is a thing to be manipulated by another. In terms now made familiar by Martin Buber, true two-way communication takes place in an "I-Thou" relationship. In such communication separateness is overcome. Hearing becomes understanding. Seeing becomes perceiving. Compassion arises because if one suffers, the other suffers also.

COMMUNICATION REGARDING GOD

Communication between one person and another regarding human predicament, divine revelation, or man's encounter with God may take place in either of the two ways we have just been describing. Consider that fact with especial reference to communication regarding God.

This may be one-way communication, in which pressure is exerted by one person to get another to feel or act or believe in a certain way. It is not very probable that the encounter with God will be brought about as a result of the communication. For in this case God is not a Self who confronts us. Instead, we talk *about* him. He is an object to be discussed. His good qualities are praised, and certain difficulties in his character are ignored. He becomes for all the world like a commodity in the market which we are out to sell in spite of all resistance.

This is the effort to put a good face on religion and give it an appeal. Much that passes for the teaching of religion is nothing more than just such a one-way process. The human self toward whom it is directed has to resist it or forfeit his integrity. At bottom this has nothing to do with resisting God himself. It is resisting persons who claim to be acting on behalf of God but who in fact are trying to "put something over" on the object of their endeavors. Unhappily, however, resistance to the person making this effort is often confused with rejecting God himself. This is one reason why deep two-way communication is so often needed in order that the hurt caused by persons acting in the name of God may be healed.

There is a two-way communication regarding God. Here two or more persons truly participate in one another as when, for example, together they face wonder, and share in joy; or as together they face predicament, and share in concern, in despair perhaps, and in release if release should come. As this takes place, communication becomes communion. For in true two-way communication "something happens" which transforms human interaction into a spiritual medium, that is, a medium in which the grace of God is at work, and in which it is possible that God will be perceived disclosing himself.

One of the most important distinguishing marks of true two-way communication is honesty. If communication is to be more than a verbal duel between people wearing masks, there must be honesty regarding the negative as well as the positive aspects of man's response to God. *This means that true two-way communication permits doubt as well as faith to be expressed.* The importance of this point cannot be too strongly urged. For the moment when the religious community begins to make it impossible for doubt as well as faith to be expressed is the moment when that community begins to breed distrust between its members, and falsity within individual selves who must cover doubt with a show of faith.

We have just been speaking of two kinds of communication; now we must add that communication between one person and another regarding human predicament, regarding revelation, or regarding man's encounter with God *requires symbols.* In order to communicate with one another about *anything*, we must use symbols; we must do so, that is, if we wish to transcend our animal nature and claim our human nature. This is true even in the simplest matters, and as the matters of communication become more complex the importance of symbols becomes all the greater.

Some persons have come to associate symbolism with religion only. They have thought that, outside religion, people get along without symbols; and they have sometimes maintained that it would be better if we abandoned symbolism in the religious community. A view of this kind has sometimes grown up because of the abuse of symbolism in the religious community; but quite as likely it arises out of misapprehension as to the nature of symbols. *Symbols are a means of discourse wherever men communicate with one another.* We should, then, inquire further into the nature of symbols.

SYMBOLS

Both signs and symbols are means of communication.[1] Present usage varies in the meaning assigned to these two terms. Here we use "sign" as the broader of the two. A sign in this broad sense is anything which serves as a means of communication. Thus for example a sign may be a mark of some kind, such as an arrow pointing in a certain direction; it may be a sound uttered with a particular tone or inflection, such as "hmm" uttered with a rising or a falling inflection. It may be a word, it may be a gesture, and so on. A sign stands for something else, and thus points beyond itself.

For present purposes we may think of signs as falling into three classes: arbitrary signs, icons, and symbols. An arbitrary sign is one to which a meaning is assigned, but the sign has little or no discernible meaning in itself. Examples are letters of the alphabet, and certain characters used in mathematics, such as + and −.

An icon is a visible image of some object, especially of a person. The actual appearance of the person may be completely unknown, but the icon "stands for" his presence; as for example, an icon of Jesus, or of the Virgin Mary, or of a saint.

A symbol is a sign representing something else to which it points; it represents that to which it points, not because it has been arbitrarily chosen for that purpose, but because it is intrinsically related to it in some way, such as by association with it, or participation in it.

Of these three, the arbitrary sign, the icon, and the symbol, the symbol has by far the greatest importance in Biblical and theological thought, and in our communication with one another regarding predicament, revelation, and encounter. Arbitrary signs have an interest for those who pursue the specialized study of languages, inscriptions, ancient coins, and so on, which were means of communication but which are of remote concern when it comes to ordinary communication in the Christian community. As for the icon, its value is definitely negated in the Bible: "Thou shalt not make unto thee any graven image." The tremendous invective in the Bible against idolatry means, among other things, that man's direct representation of God was *not* the medium through which God confronted man.

With the symbol, the case is notably different. *In the Biblical record of revelation, symbols make up the language through which God discloses himself to man.* Thus Biblical symbols take on primary importance for the understanding of God's revelation to man, and man's encounter with God. But before proceeding to discuss and exemplify the Biblical symbols still further, we should state certain characteristics of the symbol as such.

1. As defined, a symbol is a sign pointing beyond itself to something which it represents because associated with it, or participating in it.

2. That which the symbol represents cannot be grasped by the ordinary use of the senses.

3. The symbol represents a meaning which it would be difficult or impossible to communicate in nonsymbolic terms.

4. A symbol refers ultimately to that which cannot be expressed in the ordinary terms of time and space.

5. A symbol is not arbitrarily chosen to represent that to which it refers. Rather, it is inwardly and organically related to that to which it refers. This means that the symbol is rooted in some historical situation or event, or in something so familiar to people as to be a matter of common knowledge. This further means that the symbol is rooted in a community, that it carries undertones and overtones of meaning, and that it can be used as a means of communication in the community where it has its roots.

6. Symbols are freely drawn from the common life. The

imagery of symbols drawn from such sources may have profound significance for faith. Thus the parables of Jesus, illuminating the meaning of the Kingdom of God, abound with imagery from nature and from the secular world.

7. The symbol is concrete. This means, among other things, that a symbol furnishes specific detail which can be apprehended by the senses, and yet at the same time it stimulates the mind to grasp the meaning which the symbol itself alone cannot fully express.

8. A symbol participates in that to which it refers. If that to which it refers has power in it, the symbol has power in it.

9. A symbol does not fully contain that to which it points. This means that the symbol is not identical with that to which it refers, and all of that to which it refers is not present in the symbol. To illustrate this, one may think of a "cone of reality," shaped like a V. The reality itself stretches away into infinity, like the openness at the top of the V. At the point of the V lies a small section which we may think of as a symbol of the entire cone of reality. As a symbol it stands for that to which it refers, it does not contain all of that reality, but participates in it. Thus:

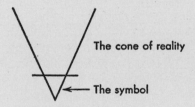

The cone of reality

The symbol

10. Although a symbol contains power, we from our side must participate in the symbol if the symbol is to yield up its power. This we begin to do when we begin to perceive that in which the symbol participates. When we begin to perceive we begin also to respond with the "Yes" or with the "No."

11. While a symbol serves to communicate meaning, yet we for our part add to the meaning which the symbol has, by our own act of responding to it. This at least is possible in a free community where the interpretation of the symbol is not authoritatively im-

posed as a condition of acceptance by the community. Actually this often takes place even in the most authoritarian community or system; but then it is regarded as rebellion or heresy.

12. A comparison between a definition and a symbol is instructive. A definition sets limits around that to which it refers; thus the classic formula for defining something is: "S is nothing but ——" In this way a definition draws the mind in, and restricts its work on that to which the definition refers. A symbol, on the other hand, sets the mind soaring out into an unbounded area, stimulates the mind to do its own work of recognizing the meaning in the symbol, and encourages the quest for further meaning.

BIBLICAL SYMBOLS

When we come to consider *Biblical* symbols we are met by two significant facts. The first is that symbolism is the language in which the reports of revelation were recorded. From beginning to end the Bible abounds in symbols. Indeed, if the symbols could be stripped out, nothing of any interest or any consequence would be left.

The other fact is that *Biblical symbols make up the basic vocabulary of communication within the Christian community*. These symbols provide a common medium of discourse regarding human predicament, divine revelation, and man's encounter with God. This is true within one Christian community where people meet face to face. It is true also of the Christian church throughout the world. These symbols are the one common language of Christian faith in all places, and in all ages of the Christian era.

When the symbolism of the Bible is lost from the vocabulary of the Christian community there remains no common medium of communication regarding the predicaments of men or the salvation of God. The language to describe tribulation then becomes a private language in which a man tries to express his woes, but his neighbor does not understand. Many saviors are proclaimed, but only to little esoteric circles.

Like other symbols, Biblical symbols can be used either in one-way or in two-way communication. There is no need to elaborate the point that they can be used in a system of one-way pressures. It is more important to observe that *Biblical symbols by their own nature are evocative, designed to draw forth a response of some kind; and this in turn can set up an interaction which is actually a two-way communication.*

As a prelude to two-way communication the Biblical symbols may call forth any or all of the classic responses of curiosity, wonder, surprise, and incredulity. Curiosity to know what a symbol means is recognized in the Bible itself as a natural starting point for the teaching of the meaning of the symbol. For curiosity stirs up the initial question, "What is this?" That kind of question is specifically mentioned as the beginning of communication regarding the passover meal, the redemption rites, and memorial markers.[2] Wonder can be the beginning of adoration, and surprise can be the beginning of new disclosures through something already familiar.

The religious value of incredulity in the presence of the symbol must not be overlooked. Facing the symbol it often comes about that man breaks forth in some response of protest or of rejection. "I don't see it" and "I can't take that" are common responses of incredulity. The Bible abounds in responses of incredulity before the symbols that bring some disclosure. But commonly the response of incredulity is not beaten down; rather it is honored as the opening into further disclosure or further perception.

All of these, curiosity, wonder, surprise, and incredulity, are the beginnings of two-way communication. For the symbol has called forth some kind of question, and the question is the first movement of the self into that dialogue of two-way communication in which man participates in the symbol and in which, it may be, he encounters God.

SYMBOLS OF ENCOUNTER

Having spoken of symbols in general terms, we should now consider some of the actual symbols that are used in the Bible. The symbols that are to be found there are so numerous, however, that it would be impossible to deal with all of them in a book of this kind. For present purposes some principle of selection must be found, and an obvious one offers itself.

We have already said that the principal purpose in using the Bible in the Christian community is the purpose of the continuing encounter. Accordingly we may now select symbols that are closely connected with confrontation and encounter as reported or considered in the Bible. Such symbols illuminate man's encounter with God because they represent some aspect of God's disclosure of himself to man and some aspect of man's perception of that disclosure or his response to it. For the sake of convenience these may be called symbols of encounter.

In the lists that follow we shall distinguish a number of classes of symbols of encounter. In general we proceed from the more simple to the more complex types. In no case is there an attempt to list all the symbols of a given class. Usually no references are cited, as this would clutter the material unnecessarily. Any one wishing to see instances of the use of a particular symbol can readily locate references in any good concordance.

OBJECTS

One class of symbols consists of objects of various kinds. These are concrete *things*. Some, such as bread, are drawn directly out of the common life. Others, such as an altar, are fashioned from things drawn out of the common life but set aside to some purpose closely associated with man's encounter with God. The objects are such as these (reading down, not across):

Blood	Shrine
Wine	Tent (tabernacle)
Bread	Ark of the covenant
Tables	Altar
Book	Laver
Tears	Water
Stones	Incense
House	Animals (lamb, etc.)
Ladder	Fortress
Footstool	Hiding place
Feathers	Sword

FORCES OF NATURE

In a preceding chapter it was observed that physical nature is perceived in the Bible as a medium of revelation. In actual discourse this perception becomes very specific, as this partial list will show. Two observations need to be made. One is that some symbols need to be repeated in more than one class. Water is an example. The other is that the forces of nature as Biblically perceived symbolize hostile power, and indifference, as well as beneficent power. The friendly and dependable universe so beloved by romantics is not a true transcript of Biblical symbolism any more than it is of personal experience. Symbols of encounter are drawn from such forces of nature as:

Life	Night	Sun
Fertility	Eclipse	Stars
Sterility	Dawn	Storm
Barrenness	Sunrise	Wave
Childbirth	Morning	Rain
Growth	Evening	Dew
Healing	Wind	Cloud
Health	Breath	Snow
Strength	Blood	Hail
Weakness	Fire	Drought
Sickness	Water	Plague, unspecified
Death	Sea	Locusts
Light	River	Flies
Darkness	Flood	Earthquake

Fermentation ("leaven")

PERSONS IN A ROLE

Different aspects of selfhood in God or in Jesus Christ are symbolized by some of the roles which persons in the common life sustain to one another. Symbols of this kind include such as:

The king	The potter
The ruler	The builder

The judge	The watchman
The prince	The father
The shepherd	The mother
The farmer (sower)	The son
The vinedresser	The brother
The husbandman	The friend
The adoptive father	

FEELINGS, EMOTIONS, SENSATIONS

The range of common feelings, emotions, and sensations provide another body of symbols. These gain their value because they are associated with, or participate in, qualities in God which are known by encounter. The first column refers to qualities in God which are symbolized by positive feelings and emotions; the second, to qualities in God symbolized by negative feelings and emotions; while the third refers to negative feelings and emotions inspired in man by some Self-disclosure of God.

Love	Anger	Fear
Yearning	Hate	Trembling
Compassion	Jealousy	Dread
Mercy	Wrath	Horror
Peace	Rejection	Fleeing
Acceptance		

UNREHEARSED, SPONTANEOUS ACTION

There is a large number of unrehearsed, spontaneous actions used to symbolize "action" by God. These may include any action appropriate to any role, such as father, king, shepherd, and judge. Spontaneous action appears in almost innumerable forms. This list illustrates:

Speaking	Healing
Refusing to speak	Hallowing
Making	Blessing
Breaking	Thwarting
Remarking	Illuminating

Mending
Commanding
Giving laws
Teaching
Asking a question
Answering a question
Refusing to answer a question
Hearing
Seeing
Smelling
Watching
Knowing
Searching for
Finding
Planting
Rooting up
Giving the increase

Confusing
Chiding
Testing
Weighing
Waiting
Going out to meet
Rebuking
Shielding
Punishing
Rewarding
Casting down
Raising up
Laughing in derision
Remembering
Forgetting
Putting a stumbling block
Sending a messenger

Demanding an accounting

RITUALIZED ACTION

This type of action may once have been spontaneous, but when we meet it it has been reduced to ritual. Generally speaking, ritualized action symbolizes some aspect of the encounter between man and God, but the action itself tends to become stereotyped. Commonly the details of the action are closely prescribed, although this is not always the case. When closely prescribed, the details themselves tend to take on symbolic significance. When not closely prescribed the details of the action may be settled by some form of ecclesiastical legislation, or else they may remain the subject of long debate. Actions of the ritualized kind are such as:

Offering sacrifice
Wearing special garments during ministration
Washing in special purification before ministration

Avoidance of contact with the "unclean"
Rites of purification after childbirth, menstruation, and other sexual functions

Rites of purification after contact with the dead, and other "unclean" objects
Circumcising
Baptizing
Anointing with oil
Burning incense
Eating a memorial meal
Breaking bread
Holding up one's hands
Holding up another's hands
Reading Scripture
Preaching ("heralding")
Teaching
Praying
Kneeling in prayer
Falling on the face in prayer
Singing
Mourning
Putting ashes on the head
Rending the garments
Dancing "before the Lord"
Going in procession

Speaking with tongues
Ecstatic "prophesying"
Keeping holy days of rest
Keeping holy days and seasons of celebration
Keeping holy days of celebration (e.g., Jubilee)
Paying tithes
Giving alms
Making freewill offerings
Allowing the land to rest
Causing land titles to revert
Setting slaves free
Fleeing for sanctuary ("laying hold of the horns of the altar")
Observing dietary laws
Fasting
Feasting
Revering symbols of symbols, such as the cross, the blood, the altar, the bread, the cup, and the phylactery

THE NAME

In the Bible great importance is attached to "the name." This is true as regards Deity, as regards man, and as regards places. As for Deity, several points deserve attention. In the first place, the name by which God is known is regarded in the Old Testament as being a matter of utmost significance. Actually he is known by many names, especially El, Elohim, El Shaddai, and Jahweh. Each of these carries some different shade of meaning. But the distinctive name of Israel's God is Jahweh. A crucial aspect of Jahweh's disclosure of himself is the account of the disclosure of his name.[3]

In the second place, the name of God stands for the character of God. It is a symbol of what he himself is. The name is regarded as participating in what God himself is. Accordingly, to honor or to profane the name of God is to render reverence or contempt to God himself, that is, to what he himself is in his essence.

A third point to be observed is that in the New Testament "the name" of Jesus holds a place corresponding in importance to that which is given to the name of Jahweh in the Old Testament. His "name" stands for what he himself is, both in his character as a person, and in his relationship to the Father. So the "name" of Jesus is to receive universal homage;[4] and his disciples are to pray "in the name" of Jesus, not as a magic formula to gain power, but rather as a token of striving to participate in the spirit of him whose name is used.

Importance is also attached to the name given to a man. The name stands for unique individuality, so that by his name an individual is forever lifted out of the undifferentiated mass of humanity and stands as a responsible being facing his Maker. And the name stands for the personal character of that individual so that again the name seems to be regarded as participating in what one is.

A great many personal names in the Bible stand as symbols of encounter with God in the sense that parents gave a child a name which signified some crisis in the parents' life, or signified some hope which they entertained for the child's character. This kind of meaning is communicated by the structure of a personal name. Especially interesting is the way in which the name of God enters the name of man. Thus it is obvious in reading personal names in the Bible that many of them contain the syllables *el*, *iah*, and *jah*. These are simply syllables standing for the name of Deity, incorporated into the name of man or woman. The *el* of course is the *El* which means God; and the *iah* or *jah* stands for Jahweh. Thus the name Elijah means "My God is Jahweh"; the name Adonijah means "My Lord is Jahweh"; Eliel means "God is God," and so on.

As for places, the names of localities commonly convey meaning, and often stand as symbols of some kind of encounter with God. Thus Bethel means "House of God," Ebenezer means "stone of help," Peniel means "face of God," and so on. Many narratives in the Bible explain the origin of such place names.

THE NEW NAME

The concept of newness, prominent in the Bible, is used to symbolize the results of the redemptive and re-creative acts of God. This is well illustrated by the symbol of "the new name." Just as the name symbolizes the character of the person, so the new name symbolizes what one becomes when he is re-created by the power of God. The new name stands for the new man. It is a symbol of the new self.

The new name, or at least newness itself, is not restricted to persons. There is a new covenant in place of the old. There is a new Jerusalem to serve as a habitation for those who themselves are made new. And as if to symbolize the fact that there is a hope which leaves nothing out of its blessed vision, there is a new earth and even a new heaven.

THE STORY OF A MARVEL

There is a type of story in the Bible which recounts some aspect of man's encounter with God, but which contains elements of high improbability. The story relates events quite unlike those that take place in ordinary experience. And just because the events described *are* so different from those of the common life, *the reader himself encounters something about which he has to come to a decision.* He has to decide what this kind of material says to him as an individual. And as a member of a Christian community he often has to decide whether he can consent to admit this kind of material into the system of communication which the community uses in its education of the young, or whether on the other hand he will try to have it excluded.

Several possibilities are open. One of these is to avoid this kind of material altogether in the curriculum, because of the difficulties which it presents. This course of action is not uncommon, and it is easy to understand why it should be chosen. Are not all religions full of tales of the miraculous? What distinguishes these stories from a thousand others like them, to be found in the source materials of the history of religions? Has not the scientific outlook made it impossible to credit stories of miraculous intervention in the natural course of events? For reasons of this kind many have felt impelled to remove from the system of communication everything that tells of supernatural intervention in the course of nature or in human affairs.

But however strong the reasons for excluding the stories of the marvel, what is left after these have been censored out is really not the Bible at all. We then have on our hands a document that has been radically tampered with. It may be more respectable intellectually, but something it was trying to tell us has been suppressed when the story of the marvel is taken out. And yet—and yet—what are we to do with these stories in an age of science?

Another possibility is to regard the stories of the marvel as records which must be understood literally, because they are contained in the Bible. Such a view, however, binds one with a double obligation. He must defend the possibility of a miracle, and he must defend particular miracles as facts of history. Many consider this the only honest way in which the Biblical stories of marvel can be regarded.

But it is a common experience for modern man, brought up in this view of the Bible, to find that it places on faith a burden too grievous to be borne. That such a view of the Biblical stories of the marvel is an incubus to many seems to be attested by the large number of persons who make this the target when they revolt against religion.

A third possibility is to regard the stories as description, not of a breach of the laws of nature, but rather as recounting some unique combination of natural events. In some cases this proves helpful by giving a natural explanation for some event which gains its importance just because it occurred in the ordinary course of nature. But even this approach sometimes proves to be a dubious gift, making the religious value of some narrative depend upon the results of archaeological or astronomical research.

A fourth possibility is to treat these stories, or at least many of them, as myths. When this is done the value of the stories lies in their symbolism. Through symbols they communicate meanings which defy any other means of communication. Viewing the Biblical stories of marvels as being primarily symbolic in character has brought a feeling of deliverance to many who have understood that we cannot prune out these stories of marvel without doing violence to that which the writers of the Bible were trying to communicate, who are not willing to take up the burden of defending the stories as literal in every detail, but who have no difficulty in reckoning with the myth as a means of communicating regarding some of the most profound aspects of reality. There are those, however, who are offended by the very word "myth" as applied to anything in the Bible.

In the face of such alternatives no choice is free of serious difficulties. This very fact, it may well be, is part of the genius of communicating through this type of material. There is nothing abstract, nothing self-evident, nothing tame, about these stories. They stir up questions at once and compel some decision as to the way we for our part shall respond, whether with the "Yes" of wonder and surprise, or with the "No" of incredulity and rejection. To that extent, then, they are symbols and serve as means of communication, no matter how we regard them. They say something to which we have to give some kind of response.

The stories of marvel include such narratives as these:

> The temptation and fall of man in the garden of Eden
> The flood and the saving of a remnant in the ark
> The confusion of tongues at the tower of Babel
> The plagues upon the Egyptians
> The crossing of the Red Sea
> The feeding of the people with quails and manna
> The crossing of the Jordan
> The fall of Jericho
> Joshua commanding the sun to stand still
> Gideon's fleece
> The call of the child Samuel
> The recall of Samuel from the dead
> The ascent of Elijah in the fiery chariot
> The men in the fiery furnace
> Nebuchadnezzar's downfall and recovery

The handwriting on the wall
The temptation of Jesus
The transfiguration of Jesus
Stilling a storm
Walking on the sea
Multiplying the loaves and fishes
Stories of the raising of the dead
Tongues of fire at Pentecost
Opening of prison doors

THE APPEARANCE

The Bible contains many accounts of the Self-disclosure of God to man by means of the appearance of Jahweh or "the angel of Jahweh." Commonly the accounts of these theophanies are expressed in terms of manifestation to the senses. The encounter thus is described as an experience of seeing, hearing, entering into dialogue, and so on. Generally speaking, as one moves from the earlier to the later portions of the Bible the concreteness of detail in the theophanies diminishes, and the glory of God becomes more prominent in the descriptions. Accounts of theophany include such instances as:

The dialogue with Jahweh God in the garden
The angel of Jahweh to Hagar
Jahweh appearing to Abraham, who sees three men[5]
The angel of Jahweh "in a flame of fire out of the midst of a bush," to Moses
Jahweh to Moses at Sinai, revealing his goodness, his glory, but not "my face"[6]
The Shekinah, the shining glory, "that which dwells" above the ark in the Holy of Holies
The pillar of fire and cloud in the wilderness
The captain of the host of Jahweh, to Joshua
The glory of Jahweh filling the temple[7]
The overpowering glory of the transfiguration

SUPERNATURAL BEINGS

Various personal beings of a supernatural order are mentioned in the Bible. Some of these, as cherubim and seraphim, angels, and the archangel, are pictured as wholly obedient to the will of God and as serving that will. It is difficult to distinguish between "the angel of Jahweh" as a term for Jahweh himself, and an "angel," who literally is one sent, a messenger.[8] Similarly it is often difficult to draw any distinction between "the angel" of God and "the Spirit" of God. Both "angel" and "spirit" symbolize God's personalized forthgoing in action.

Other supernatural beings are referred to, such as Satan, the dragon, demons, evil spirits, and the like. They are hostile to God and inimical to man. They symbolize personalized will in the universe, actively in rebellion against the will of God and bent on defeating that will. They express in personal symbols what may be called a limited dualism, that is, a view of the universe as the scene of titanic conflict between good and evil. But the good and the evil are not abstract principles. In the Biblical symbols they stand forth as powers in personal form arrayed against each other.

THE PERSON

An individual man may stand as a symbol of encounter; or more accurately, as a symbol of that which is encountered through him. His own response to what *he* encountered survives in the religious heritage, so that "he, being dead, yet speaketh." Thus Abraham, himself faithful, stands as the father of the faithful and in him one encounters faithfulness. Moses, giver of law, comes to stand for the law. Elijah, champion of Jahweh in the midst of devotion to Baal, stands as "the prophet." David becomes a symbol of poetry, of kingship, and of a friendship with God which overcomes personal sinfulness.

In contrast to such men, the historian of Israel never tires of referring to "Jeroboam the son of Nebat who made Israel to sin." The mere names of all these men and their kind take on a freightage of meaning; as when in the story of the transfiguration it is told that Jesus "talked with" Moses and Elijah, and then supplanted them so that he and he only was to be seen.

Again, there is a class of passages which refer to encounter with God in terms of Spirit. In general these passages refer to the Spirit as power which is personal in nature, power which participates in the character of God, power which goes forth from God to do his will, and is infused into man so that man is empowered. Thus, the Spirit "comes upon" a man. The Spirit speaks to a man, and directs him. The Spirit "clothes himself with" a man,[9] as if putting on human garments. The Spirit takes possession of a man, or fills a man. Such terms all symbolize God's forthgoing with power, toward man or into man. And man for his part may be "in the Spirit," so that personal interpenetration is symbolized; God imparting himself in power, man participating in power.

The doctrine of the Incarnation presents Jesus Christ as the unique instance of the person in whom and through whom God is perceived. The encounter with him is expressed in various symbols. He is perceived as the Christ, and is so confessed. He is perceived as Lord, and this it appears is the earliest form of confessing him. He is perceived as the Logos, or Word of God, who "was made flesh and dwelt among us." To encounter him was to encounter God, as is expressed in the saying, "He that hath seen me hath seen the Father." And his actions in reconciling men to God were God's actions, as when in Pauline terms it is said, "God was in Christ, reconciling the world unto himself."

After the days of his flesh the doctrine of the Spirit becomes in great part a doctrine of the Spirit of Christ. In this way it is affirmed that the presence and the power of Jesus Christ are continuous. The resurrection expresses the deathlessness of that presence and power. The ascension and the session at the right hand of God symbolize his universality and his timelessness.

THE EVENT

The event is the historical occurrence. It is a fact of history, plus the meaning which is perceived in the fact itself. As history it is subject to examination by any and all methods which history as a science uses. If it claims to be history it can claim no exemption from the most searching investigation into its historicity. As occurrence it is concrete, specific, unrepeatable. As heritage, it belongs to all who feel that "this is ours."

An event may be perceived as revelatory. Certain events take on special significance as revelatory events because they are perceived as having two characteristics. For one thing, they disclose God's redemptive purpose and power in a unique manner at a crucial moment in history. The moment itself was a moment of dire need: "A Syrian ready to perish was my father."[10] And a second characteristic is that they are events whose redemptive significance man may appropriate *now*, affirming the same divine purpose and participating in the same divine power which the original events disclosed. To perceive them thus is to perceive them in faith.

Revelatory events can be called symbolic because they are perceived as disclosing the divine purpose and the divine power at a specific time of human predicament; because we for our part participate in that predicament; and because we may by faith participate in that which was disclosed through the original revelatory event.

In the Old Testament some of the classic instances of revelatory events which become symbols are:

> The call of Abraham to leave his homeland and become the father of the people of the covenant
> The deliverance of Israel from bondage in Egypt
> The establishing of the covenant
> The tragedy of the collapse of the nation
> The return of the exiles and the reestablishing of the community of the covenant

In the New Testament the unique revelatory events lie in the life, the suffering, the death, and the resurrection of Jesus Christ. Here faith perceives the purposes and the power of God disclosed as in no other way. Here the new covenant is opened to the whole world for appropriation and participation.

THE RELIGIOUS COMMUNITY

The religious community is both the scene and the symbol of encounter. It is the scene of encounter because it is made up of the people of the covenant who are called out from the world by God to come into togetherness with him and with one another. When they come together, as for worship, they are confronted by the living God. The community of faith thus is the community of the continuing encounter.

And the religious community itself becomes a symbol, both witnessing to, and standing for, the encounter with God. It is the congregation *of the Lord;* it is the church *of God* or *of Christ,* signifying that the living God is its sovereign, signifying also that in this community God confronts man. This double aspect of lordship and encounter is symbolized in the classical names for the places of assembly, thus:

> The tabernacle is "the tent of meeting"
> The temple is "a house of prayer," i.e., a house of fellowship with God
> The synagogue is a house where the congregation meet together to be confronted by the law and the prophets, and to pray
> The church is the "body of Christ," a living organism of which Christ is the head; made up of persons who are called out of the world into fellowship with God.

THE WORD

The word serves as a means of communication from person to person. It presupposes a self who utters and another self who can perceive meaning in what is uttered. There is a speaker, and there is a hearer. Such commonplace facts set the stage for the unique importance attached to "the word" in the Biblical accounts of communication between God and man. This is *personal* communication which is being described, personal to the point of incredible vividness.

For in the Bible "the word" is the word of *God* and God is the God who speaks. Hence that which is communicated to man in the revelatory act is often called simply "the word of the Lord." Thus one of the most common of the formulas is, "Jahweh spake to ——, saying, ——"; and another like it is, "The word of the Lord came to ——, saying, ——." And since the word presupposes man who hears as well as God who speaks, hearing comes to have high symbolical significance, as in the "Hear, O Israel," of the Shema,[11] or the injunction of Jesus, "He that hath ears to hear, let him hear."

In the Christian community, in a new sense and more profoundly than ever before, "the word" becomes the means of communication from God to man through the incarnation. In that act the Word which God uttered is a Person. Jesus Christ is perceived as the Logos, or Word, of God. The Word thus is the thrusting point of revelation, that is, of God's disclosure of himself to man. When revelation is expressed in terms of light shining into darkness, the revelatory significance of the Person as the Word is summed up in the saying, "in him was life, and the life was the light of men."[12]

"The word" comes to stand for the record of revelation. In this usage the Bible, containing the record of that which was communicated, is often called "the Word of God." This is a derived, but important, meaning of the word. For this record becomes a vehicle through which the symbols of revelatory communication are conveyed throughout the generations and uttered afresh in each generation to the members of the Christian community. Paul expresses this dynamic character of the word by saying, "Faith comes by hearing, and hearing by the word of God."[13]

The word is also the vehicle for man's response to revelation, in the two-way communication which takes place in the Christian community as the symbols of revelation confront the members of the community. If the community can endure deep honesty of feeling and expression, then the words that spring "out of the fullness of the heart" utter the "Yes" and the "No" of man's response to the revelatory symbols.

The community in which such communication can go on must set great store by the ability to communicate with one another regarding man's predicament and God's redemption. By the same token they must set an equally great value upon the ability to communicate with those who stand outside the Christian community; for that which is to be communicated is Gospel, and if those who stand within the Christian fellowship cannot communicate with those who stand beyond it, darkness is in the church as well as around it.

To lose the ability to communicate with one another is tragedy, as is symbolized in the story of the confusion of tongues at the tower of Babel. And the power of the divine Word to restore communication from God to man and from man to man is symbolized by the tongues of fire at Pentecost, and by the ability of every man then to hear the word in his own tongue.

The community where such communication goes on is itself the word of God. We have already pointed out that there are many symbols for the church. In a few instances the Christian community itself is called "the word." This community was a singular kind of word, a word that could grow and multiply.[14] Evidently other symbols for the church proved more suitable than this one; nevertheless the symbol of the church as the word of God is true, and richly suggestive.

THE VISION

The vision results when the mind thrusts into that which needs to be seen in a new configuration. In the vision, that new configuration confronts one. In it he encounters that which is "unseen" by the ordinary operation of the mind. He "sees" a new shape of things. This new shape is often regarded in the Bible as coming from God to man. The vision speaks to him, has something to tell him.

In some instances the vision is simply a dream when one is asleep. In the Bible the dream is taken seriously, and commonly is regarded as disclosing fresh meaning, either in things as they now are or in the shape of things yet to come. In other instances the vision is not in sleep, but comes in a time of trance or ecstasy. In still other instances the vision seems to be more like a reverie which is neither dream nor trance, but is characterized by powerful impression and great clarity of perception.

The vision, whether in or out of sleep, may be apocalyptic, in that it is revelatory. It may be eschatological, in that it has to do with last things. Or it may be both apocalyptic and eschatological.

The vision by its own nature is highly symbolical. The materials of the vision "stand for" something. The question of course always is, "Stand for what?" Thus the vision both reveals and conceals meaning. Thus, too, it serves as a medium for conveying powerful but dangerous meanings in disguise. It has often served as a sort of code for conveying harmless-looking but politically dangerous messages to members of the religious community in times of persecution.

Two kinds of meaning are frequently conveyed under the symbolism of the vision. One is the eventual outcome of the conflict between good and evil. Since this conflict as we know it in existence is highly concrete, so is the symbolism of the vision, as is abundantly illustrated in the book of Revelation. The other kind of meaning often conveyed by the symbolism of the vision is the relation between time and eternity. This too is handled in the most concrete way in such visions as have to do with the coming of the Son of Man, the coming of the day of the Lord, the coming of the kingdom of God, and the coming of the day of judgment.

CHAPTER VII

Changes in the Self

WHEN WE SOUGHT to define Christian education, we spoke of it as the attempt to participate in and guide the changes which take place in persons in their relationships with God, with the church, with other persons, with the physical world, and with oneself. In the last three chapters we have been considering revelation in relation to education, the themes of revelation in relation to human predicament, and communication through symbols which stand for some aspect of man's encounter with God. We need now to give closer attention to the "changes in persons" which take place, or may take place, within the encounter and which occupy so central a place in Christian education.

The term "changes in persons" is here used to include all that is ordinarily referred to in educational psychology as "learning." But it is a broader term than learning, and includes much that is not ordinarily denoted by "learning." Specifically, we may distinguish five kinds of changes in persons which are or properly may be of concern in the Christian community generally and in Christian education particularly. These are: physiological changes in the body, conditioned responses, learning by trial and error, learning by insight, and changes in the depths of the self, that is, the deeper changes which take place in the structure and functioning of the total self. After these kinds of changes in the self have been considered we may inquire how man's responses to God's disclosure of himself in revelation are related to the changes in the self.

CHANGES IN THE BODY

First to be noted are physiological changes in the body. Changes of a physiological kind are constantly taking place in the body, from the moment of conception until the moment of death. They are exemplified by such processes as the development of the fetus, being born, growing, maturing, becoming pubescent, the functioning of glands, reproduction, and senescence.

Physiological changes taking place in the body include two which are in contrast. One is constructive metabolism, or anabolism: the process by which food is converted into protoplasm. The other is distructive metabolism, or catabolism: the process by which protoplasm breaks down into waste. Thus metabolism, or the capacity of the body physically to regenerate itself and to grow, contains two opposing processes: one of a constructive, the other of a destructive, kind. This suggests a correspondence with other opposing motives or drives within the self, such as constructivity and destructivity.

When physiological changes are termed "physical" it is possible for certain assumptions of major significance to creep in unobserved, remain hidden from critical view, and then work much damage from their place of concealment. The assumptions are such as these. It may be assumed that physiological changes are "purely physical" and hence that they can be controlled, as far as they are subject to control at all, by "purely physical" means such as diet, sanitation, and medication. Again, it may be assumed that physiological changes go on apart from emotional, mental, or spiritual control, and hence are outside the concern of a spiritual religion. Still again it may be assumed that such concerns as bodily illness and health, hygiene and the like are the exclusive province of the specialists in such matters, and hence religion would be an intruder if it should in the modern day seek to enter these provinces.

But the development of psychosomatic medicine is one modern recognition, among many, that the human creature is a whole; and that what happens, say, in his emotions may affect his physical health and be reflected in the functioning of any of the organs of his body. This modern concept corresponds to a certain degree with a point of view which finds expression in at least three currents of Biblical thought.

One of these is the linkage in Jewish thought and practice between dietary and sanitary laws on the one hand, and the life of faith as obedience to God on the other hand. Any reader of the Old Testament knows how prominently this connection stands forth. The second is the intimate connection in the ministry of Jesus between the forgiveness of sin and the recovery of the person from ailment or disease. The third is the Pauline conception of redemption as redemption of the body. All this is only to say that in the basic literature of the Jewish and Christian faiths, a concern for these "changes in the body" is a religious, not a secular, concern.

CONDITIONED RESPONSES

There is a type of learning known as the conditioned response. The principle involved is stated by saying that any response which the creature is capable of making may become associated with ("conditioned to") any stimulus which it is capable of receiving. In its modern form the principle of conditioning was first developed in laboratories where experiments on the conditioning of reflexes were carried on by Pavlov and others, in work with animals.

The classic experiment with a hungry dog is often referred to as "the dog and the bell and the piece of meat." The formulae representing the results of this and similar experiments run along these lines. An unconditioned stimulus, such as presenting food, calls forth an unconditioned response, such as the secretion of saliva, when the animal is hungry. A conditioned stimulus, such as the ringing of a bell, may be presented along with the unconditioned stimulus. Gradually the unconditioned stimulus is withdrawn while the conditioned stimulus continues to be presented. With sufficient repetition the conditioned stimulus calls forth the unconditioned response. When this happens the unconditioned response has been "conditioned" to the conditioned stimulus instead of the unconditioned stimulus.

The principle of the conditioned response, derived from animal learning, was expanded into the field of human learning by John B. Watson and others. It was applied both to the conditioning and to the unconditioning of human responses to many kinds of stimuli. It was contended that an entire education could be constructed on the principle of the conditioned response; for what was learning but the conditioning of responses, and what was personality but the sum of our habits? For a few years this was heady wine to the educator. The potentialities of the human organism were without limit and so were the achievements possible in education. If the conditioning could be properly controlled, any desired outcome or body of outcomes could be secured.

It is now rather generally held that this is an extreme and untenable view. It is recognized commonly now that the principle of conditioned response needs to be supplemented by other principles of learning, especially by the principle of learning by insight and by the principle of changes in the depths of the self. Otherwise the mechanics of learning tend to become elevated in importance, while the selfhood of the human creature tends to be submerged or even violated. The system of education easily loses its way in the attempt to be scientific, while the teacher in such a system easily degenerates into a manipulator of the pupil, treating him as a thing to be experimented with and shaped according to some blueprint.

But all this in no way destroys the principle of the conditioned response. If the limitations upon the place and value of that principle are recognized, the principle itself yields valuable clues as to what goes on in human interaction. For example, this principle leads us to be aware that the response which a pupil makes is the response which he is learning; this actual response may be what we desire, or it may be very far from it; but in either case he is learning what he is doing. Many other implications of this principle for the process of interaction can be found.[1]

TRIAL AND ERROR

There is a type of learning known as learning by trial and error. For present purposes learning of this type is best exemplified by the results which follow the attempt to solve a problem, particularly the kind of problem which one faces in a completely unfamiliar situation. In such a case he is likely to make random responses until he perhaps hits upon a response which gives "success" or "satisfaction." He is then said to have learned by trial and error how to solve his problem.

As with conditioned responses, so here: the early experiments with trial-and-error learning were largely laboratory experiments in animal learning. Later work in educational psychology, especially work on "learning by insight," has considerably dwarfed the value of trial-and-error learning as a basis for teaching. Nevertheless, the experimental work on trial-and-error learning has yielded certain generalizations which have exerted great influence in educational theory and practice. Two results of this kind are exemplified by the laws and characteristics of learning as stated by Edward L. Thorndike, and the analysis of the process of thinking as stated by John Dewey. We may observe these very briefly.

Thorndike, working with animals, formulated certain generalizations which came to be known as "laws of learning" and "characteristics of learning."[2] His "laws of learning" embrace three items. The first is the "law of readiness" which states in effect that when any conduction unit is ready to conduct, to do so is satisfying while not to do so is annoying; and when *not* in readiness, to conduct is annoying.

The second is the "law of exercise," or of "use and disuse." The substance of this "law" is that, other things being equal, a modifiable connection between a situation and a response is strengthened by use, and is weakened by disuse. The third is the "law of effect." The substance of this "law" is that when a modifiable connection between situation and response is accompanied or followed by a satisfying state of affairs, the strength of that connection is increased; but when accompanied or followed by an annoying state of affairs, its strength is weakened.

The "characteristics of learning" represent an attempt to correct and supplement the "laws of learning." They consist of five assertions whose substance is as follows: First, both men and animals make multiple responses to the same situation. Second, a response is the product of a "set" or "attitude" in the animal, as well as being the product of an external situation. Third, some element in the situation may be prepotent in determining the response, for example, the experimenter himself. Fourth, the "law of assimilation or analogy" seems intended to recognize the transfer of learning when situations contain similar elements. Fifth, the "law of associative shifting" is only another way of stating the principle of the conditioned response.

We turn next to John Dewey's analysis of the process of thinking. That analysis is based on the assumption that thinking is a form of problem solving. Thinking is likened to a dramatic trial-and-error rehearsal in the mind when one faces a problem. Dewey believed that there are five characteristic steps or phases in thinking as problem solving—or, as he preferred to call it, in "reflective activity." These five steps, as he saw them, are in substance:

1. A felt difficulty. This is a time or a situation when one cannot "go ahead," cannot act overtly, is perplexed, inhibited; one then begins to form "ideas," i.e., substitutes for direct action, a mental rehearsal of possible ways to meet the difficulty and go ahead.
2. Locating and defining the difficulty.
3. Locating possible alternative ways of meeting the difficulty, and choosing one of these for further exploration; this is the "hypothesis."
4. Logical elaboration of the hypothesis, i.e., reasoning out its consequences, trying to see where it would take us, etc.
   Either the third step or the fourth step may require a search for further information, relevant knowledge, etc.; this is "the search for data."
5. Testing the hypothesis by action. Actually putting the hypothesis to the test, and evaluating the results. The results may verify the hypothesis, or on the contrary they may fail to do so. But in either case one has learned.[3]

These or similar steps in thinking have furnished the basis for several characteristic types of educational procedure. Two of them are especially noteworthy. One is the project, which figures largely in the literature and practice of "creative education." The other is the process of group thinking, which provided a method for refining the participation of the members of a group in problem solving. It was customary for the literature on projects to suggest that a project naturally moves through the steps of thinking as Dewey understood them; and so with the literature on group thinking.

Dewey insisted that scientific method is to be equated with thinking. Thinking, in turn, was understood as has just been summarized from his book *How We Think*. Scientific method represented for Dewey the road to truth.[4] It was the method to be used in attacking any of the problems which men face. It could be incorporated into education as the central principle in the theory of education, since this kind of "thinking" led to the only kind of "learning" regarded as worthy.[5] Thus in the schoolroom pupils were to be introduced to the use of scientific method as *the* way of taking hold of any problem, and as *the* way of arriving at truth.

If now we consider the work which has been done on the conditioning of responses and on trial-and-error learning, there are values for Christian education, but at the same time there are limitations which compel us to look still further for a more adequate conception of the changes that take place in persons.

The principle of the conditioned responses and the laws and characteristics of learning as stated by Thorndike have two factors in common. Each of these factors has its value for Christian education, but also has its limitations. One is the fact that they refer to *animal* nature. Such potentiality for change as the human creature shares with the rest of the animal creation is illuminated by this type of work. Specifically, where habits are under consideration the findings in this type of experimentation are likely to have relevance.

But where human potentiality transcends that of the rest of the animal creation, little or no light is shed by this kind of experimentation, on the changes which take place in persons. To put it oversimply, we share a very great deal in common with the animal world, and in many things we learn as they learn. But in proportion as we are concerned with the more distinctively *human* components in the human self, the more sobering is our plight if we must seek self-understanding by turning to the mind of the rat for illumination.

Another common factor running through work of this kind is a tendency to approach the learner from the outside, as if he had no interior life over which *he* held command. He seems to be thought of as an organism responding to external stimuli, and not as an "I" who is self-conscious and self-determining. The will of the learner is forgotten.

The external stimuli which play upon the learner are seen as the forces that move him. They are his "motivation" for change. And in so far as this is the case the teacher is left with the problem of supplying motivation from outside the pupil; that is, the teacher must supply the stimuli which will do something to the pupil and get him to respond in the desired way. These two common factors mean that when psychologies go this far but can go no further the sense of sharing in animal nature is strong, but the sense of human selfhood is almost completely lost. This situation, when prolonged and unrelieved, becomes a modern form of the predicament of mis-apprehension, to which the theme of creation is directed.

As for Dewey's work, its influence has been great not only in the public schools but in Christian education as well. As far as changes in persons are concerned it has signal value in at least two respects. One is the importance attached to the individual's *own* experience in the learning process, as compared with secondhand experience which someone else purveys to him. The other is the importance attached to the *sharing* of experience, so that learning becomes a social experience. Both these values stand as good in their own right; and, incidentally, are very close to the human side of the New Testament conception of knowing by experience within the *koinonia.*

Dewey's philosophy has two especially severe limitations, however, as far as changes in persons are concerned. One is his inability to deal with the demonic element in the human creature and in human society. This demonic element, whatever one may wish to call it, is a fact in the world of observable experience to which he was strangely oblivious. In so far as he recognized this element at all, he thought it could be overcome by the use of man's intelligence. He thus fell into the ancient error of believing that the way to triumph over the irrational is to be more rational; not seeing that this faith is perhaps the most irrational credulity of which man is capable. Such lack of realism is almost incredible in one who set such store by being scientific.

The other limitation to be noted here is the tendency to restrict "truth" to that which can be known by the use of scientific method. It is quite possible that Dewey himself misunderstood the nature of scientific method;[6] but in any event he advocated what he thought scientific method is, and a great number of people accepted both his version of what scientific method is and his conception of the relation between scientific method and truth.

Apparently the wide acceptance of the view that truth must be reached by the use of scientific method is due less to critical thinking than it is to popular awe of whatever is called "scientific." The veneration paid to "science" in the modern world is so great that when the label "scientific" is attached to a theory or to a statement, or when a method of work is alleged to be "scientific method," then the theory or the method takes on a halo, the fact becomes a gospel not open to doubt, and men bow by second nature as once they bowed when passing a shrine.

Emphasis on the pragmatic nature of truth has brought the result that many in the Christian community can think readily enough in terms of the search for truth, the discovery of truth, and reverence for truth wherever found. These are commonplace in the vocabulary of a multitude of sincere persons. But many of these same persons find that the conception of truth in the form of a Person who is seeking *them* has become obscured or even completely lost.

In further consequence, when truth is conceived as pragmatic in nature the changes in persons which are most highly prized are those that lie in the direction of *increased creativity*. Hence great stress is placed on "creative education." When this emphasis has been strong the deeper changes in the self and the conditions under which they take place have often been crowded out of the field of religious concern. A concern for creativity by the self then replaces a concern for the re-creation of the self. It is not too difficult for a skilled teacher to secure creative performance in a group of persons; and with this performance before one's eyes it has been easy to overlook the demonic element or even to deny warmly that it even exists at all.

Many persons engaged in the church's educational work entered that work fired to enthusiasm by an optimistic, idealistic conception of human nature and of the Christian society. Sooner or later this bright optimism is almost certain to be shattered by hard reality. What is to become of the disillusioned man or woman whose task in the church remains but whose dream has been proved unreal? The hour when that question comes to him is the hour when he faces and enters the predicament of the demonic element in human society, to which the theme of vocation is pointed.

LEARNING BY INSIGHT

There is yet another type of learning known as learning by insight. The formulation of principles underlying this type of learning is based on Gestalt psychology. The findings from experiments in Gestalt psychology agree generally with those drawn from experiments with conditioned responses and with trial-and-error learning, in some respects. For example, all findings from these sources emphasize the sense of need as a motive for learning, especially such elemental needs as hunger and thirst, They emphasize the importance of the memories of feelings associated with a particular stimulus or situation.

But the work done in Gestalt psychology elevates to prominence certain principles which tend to be neglected or even ignored in experimental work on learning by conditioned responses or by trial and error. Two of these need to be lifted out here for notice; namely, the principle of response to a relationship, and the principle of insight.

There is the principle of response to a relationship. In experimental work with conditioned responses and with trial-and-error learning, such as we have already noted, emphasis was laid on the learner's response to specific stimuli. In contrast, experiments in Gestalt psychology bring out and strongly emphasize the point that the learner is responding to a whole field in which the parts stand in a relationship to one another. This whole with its parts in relationship to one another makes up a Gestalt—that is, a pattern or configuration.

Thus it is sometimes said more simply that the learner responds, not to a specific stimulus, but to a relationship. In early work this Gestalt was seen as a field of inanimate parts in relationship, and the learner was seen as responding to a relationship between inanimate parts. But soon it became apparent that a group of *persons* also makes up a Gestalt. They constitute a "power field" in which the parts, that is, the individual persons, stand in a complex relationship to one another.

This being so, it was necessary to study the *relationships* of the parts in the power field to which any individual within that field responds. This study of relationships inevitably became the study of *dynamics, that is, of power functioning in the relationships between persons.* Hence light is thrown on the fundamental proposition that a source of the dynamic of change in persons is to be sought in the relationships between persons. Thus, as the dynamic operating in groups has become a field of inquiry, the strong new interest in the dynamics of human relationships has supplemented the modern inquiries into intrapsychic dynamics.

Again, there is the principle of insight. This principle is needed as a corrective of the conception of learning by trial and error. When placed in a problem situation the individual *may* "see" the solution suddenly. This means that instead of responding by random movements and finding a solution by trial and error, he *may* respond by insight and find his solution by a prompt adaptation of means to ends.

In this event he attains his goal quickly, without blundering through to chance success. He then can be said to *perceive meaning* in the situation, because the parts in the total field stand in a relationship to one another which he is capable of mentally grasping. The Gestalt, or configuration, has suddenly shifted, with the result that the sense of frustration in meaninglessness gives way to a sense of meaning perceived.

The principle of insight is of great importance in situations where moral and spiritual confusion prevail. Into such a situation a ray of light may flash, to be followed perhaps by the feeling which one expresses when he says, "Now *this* makes *sense*." Or it may be followed by a sense of being released to pursue some goal without being held back. At times the flash of insight will light up a relatively small field with new meaning for the self who perceives it. At other times the insight will penetrate so far into the total field in which the self is involved as to cause one to feel that he has entered "a new world." And at still other times the new insight will cause a shift within the self so radical as to give one the feeling and the conviction that a new self is coming into being.

When insight is followed by the feeling of seeing a new world or of being a new and different self, we are at the threshold of those "deeper changes in the self" to which we earlier referred. Indeed, one who uses such terms concerning himself probably is undergoing changes of a much deeper kind than those which we commonly refer to as "learning." The precise language of a quantitative psychology becomes less and less capable of expressing what is happening. One is obliged to turn instead to the symbolic language of poetry, music, art, and religion for terms with which he can communicate the subtleties of the new meaning.

DEEPER CHANGES

The deeper changes that take place in the self are of concern both to psychology and to religion. As for psychology, two streams of modern psychological thought appear to be capable of throwing light upon the nature of these deeper changes in the self. One of these is Gestalt psychology with its principle of relationship and its principle of insight, to which we have already referred. These principles have to do with the depths of the self in the sense that they point to the flow of power and to the shift in perception which may cause power to be released or redirected.

The other stream is that commonly known as depth psychology. This psychology, although split into many schools, is an intensely active field of work, steadily turning up fresh findings. From this source have come contributions which seem to have altered permanently our understanding of the deeper aspects of human nature, especially the unconscious.

This psychology can throw light on the nature of the changes in the depths of the self because it is discovering analytical methods for understanding how disturbances of selfhood originate and develop in the individual, and because it is refining psychotherapeutic methods for the healing of the sick self. We have already had occasion to note the generalization which is emerging from both these streams; namely, that the human self is formed in relationships; if it is de-formed, it is de-formed in relationships; and if it is re-formed, it is re-formed in relationships.

The deeper changes in the self are a concern in religion as well as in psychology. Indeed, they are religion's chief concern whenever the need for redemption is felt. For redemption is redemption of the self; and if this is not conceived as a merely mechanical rescue it points to changes in the self which is being redeemed. Any system of profound religious thought wrestles with the problem of these deeper changes in the self, inquiring particularly along two lines: What is the nature of these deeper changes, and how are they brought about?

Religious thought approaches those questions from the point of view of relationships. In doing so, a kinship between psychological and theological thought is indicated; both are concerned with relationships. But religious thought attempts to reckon, not merely with the present moment and the actors who are visible in the present scene, but with the totality of being. Hence in religious thought "relationships" are conceived in a cosmic frame of reference. Thus when it is said that the deeper changes take place in relationships, the statement refers not only to relationships with other human beings, but also to the relationship with God.[7]

When we inquire into the nature of the deeper changes in the self, we may consider this principle: *As man encounters God, the nature of the responses which the human self makes to the divine Self indicates the nature of the changes taking place in the depths of the self.* As a way of examining the principle, some of its implications may be observed.

The first is that we are concerned with changes that take place *within the encounter between selves.* The living God confronts the human self, and discloses himself. To this Self-disclosure man in some way responds. He is spoken to; he must answer. The encounter is a personal transaction. Thus we are basically concerned here with the changes brought about in the human creature in response to revelation.

In the second place *the responses which are made point to the changes taking place in the relationship* between the one who speaks and the one who answers. We can see the analogy in human relationships, where the response of one self to another tells the story of what is happening between them. Thus for example they may move toward each other, into greater closeness; or they may move apart into greater distance from each other. They may seal off some parts of the self from each other, while continuing to communicate in other parts of the self. Or they may freeze their relationship so that it neither grows nor diminishes.

So it is in the relation between the self and God. As God confronts man in Self-giving, the responses of man within the encounter are the outward and visible signs of the inward and invisible changes which are taking place.

As we have repeatedly pointed out, these responses may be of the accepting or of the rejecting type. These are man's "Yes" and his "No" to God. The "No," however, is not to be thought of as necessarily constituting a final act of rejection on man's part. It may be that, of course, in particular instances where an individual seals himself off against God forever.

But it is always possible that the "No" may be the utterly sincere expression of genuine doubt, which is not a final "No" but is a cry from the night of a soul which is on the road to the morning. In any case the "No" should always be heard as a response which the Christian community can contain, as long as the Spirit is truly present and participant, and as long as the one uttering the "No" does not eject himself from the community to find his own place elsewhere.

A third implication is that the nature of the changes taking place *cannot be stated with precision, but can only be inferred.* When there are changes in the character of the responses, we infer that there are changes in the character of the self. But the structure of the individual's selfhood is not open to direct observation, either by himself or by others. Its functioning, however, *is* open to observation, as when one feels within himself that he is different, or seems different to others. In that event there are grounds for inferring that changes are under way, or have already taken place.

A fourth implication is that the nature of the changes in the self which underlie changed responses *can be expressed only in symbolical terms*. A rich array of symbolical terms exists for use in referring to the results of a radical shift in the structure of the self, such as the new self, the new being, the new creature, the new heart, the new birth, the second birth, waking from sleep, and rising from the dead. Persons who are undergoing deep change produce symbolic terms of this kind quite spontaneously, and without any tutoring.

So long as such terms are understood to be symbolical, they serve remarkably well as means of communication regarding the profound events of the inner life. But the moment they begin to be viewed as literal, or as precise designations, they begin to be misleading; because what they stand for becomes obscured by the symbol itself.

A fifth implication is that *there is a region of mystery in the human self*, quite as truly as there is a region of mystery in God. This must not be understood as suggesting that there is a limit upon the right to investigate, or upon the duty to report what is found. To say that there is mystery does not mean that we are held back from inquiring into it by any and all methods at command.

To say there is mystery does mean that reverence for human life is incumbent upón all who work with it. This reverence for life can be lost in religious work just as it can in any other form of work. To say that there is mystery means also that as long as mystery remains it is a legitimate field for speculation, but not for dogma. Both in psychology and in religion the field of mystery in the human self, which should have been kept open as a field for speculation, has proved to be tempting field for dogma. Frequently these dogmas have been asserted with great aggressiveness.

In psychology a notable instance is the dogmas that have

grown up as to the unconscious. In theology a notable instance of speculation as to the nature of the deeper changes in the self is the large body of speculation regarding regeneration which has hardened into dogma.

In the case of psychology, dogma concerning therapy is erected on dogma concerning the unconscious. Not infrequently these dogmas as to the one correct therapy are pronounced with all the assurance of one who preaches a crusade. In the case of theology, dogmas regarding the communication of grace are erected on dogmas as to the nature of regeneration, and it is possible for Christians to excommunicate each other on the ground of these dogmas.

A sixth implication is that in the Christian community *we may participate with one another in response to revelation, and in the resulting changes in persons and in relationships.* This indeed is one of the marks of the *koinonia*, that we do so participate with one another in response to God. And as has been pointed out in defining Christian education, the educational work of the church is an attempt not only to participate in, but also to give guidance to, the changes which take place within the encounter.

A final implication is that *the Spirit of God is present and participant in the interaction between selves within the* KOINONIA. Whether perceived as the Spirit of God or as the Spirit of Christ, God continues to impart himself in love and in power to those who respond with the "Yes" to his disclosure of himself.

It remains now to call attention to one further point. In considering the responses of the self within the encounter it is well to distinguish between accustomed responses which have become more or less habitual, and new responses which the self has not hitherto been able to make. As for the accustomed responses, it is to be expected that, other things being equal, the accustomed situation will call forth the accustomed responses. Habit thus becomes an ally of the good, and yet at the same time it threatens to become the enemy of the better.

The story of religion is full of instances where habits set up under the religious sanction have indeed yielded certain gains, and yet have served also to prevent the divine confrontation from breaking up the shell of impoverished religious customs which one has woven around himself to keep himself from being disturbed. Often this state of things passes for "peace of mind," and whatever disturbs it is viewed as a danger to religion. Hence any efforts in Christian education which set out to "build habits" need to be kept under constant, constructive criticism.

As for the new responses which the self makes within the encounter, it is these especially which point to *changes* in the self, as compared with accustomed responses which are repeated. We seem justified in saying that one purpose of divine confrontation is to continue to produce new responses. God in his Self-giving is constantly calling the self forward into newness and toward wholeness.

At times the new responses will wear the aspect of growth along lines already taken. They are new in that they go further in a direction which is already being followed. At other times, however, the new responses will be of a revolutionary kind such as the self has never been able to produce before. In many instances the changes in the self are revolutionary in that the direction itself is new. The absolute "No" to God has changed to the unconditional "Yes." This constitutes what is properly to be called a radical conversion.

But there is a great body of changes in the self for which neither the term "growth" nor the term "conversion" is satisfactory. Growth suggests a rather unbroken upward advance, while conversion suggests an abrupt about-face. A great number of persons in the Christian life fit neither category. If categories have any value at all in such matters, it would be better to say that these persons pass through many revolutionary changes in the self during the course of a lifetime. This may always have been true, but perhaps it is especially frequent now when so many persons must pass so many times through so many radical shifts in the total pattern which life presents.

In any case the self is confronted by the living God not once only, but an endless number of times during his pilgrimage from

infancy onward. In each of these confrontations he must answer
with his "Yes" or his "No." Perhaps this fact of the continuing
encounter offers the reason why the Bible has so little to say about
conversion, and so much to say about repentance; for repentance is
a "change of mind."

CHAPTER VIII

The Dynamics of Becoming

WE BEGAN THIS book by considering the human self with its potentialities, but existing under threats which stir up anxiety because
selfhood itself is being undermined. We have considered revelation as the movement of the divine Self toward the human self in
redemptive Self-disclosure. We have observed that the scene of
this redemptive Self-disclosure of God to man is the scene where
fellowship exists, and we have observed that it is the inherent
nature of the Christian church to be the scene of just such redemptive fellowship. We have considered the themes of revelation as
expressed in the Bible, the human responses to those themes, and
the redemptive changes which can take place in the depths of the
self as the self responds to God.

There remains a group of questions to be asked regarding the
human side of this encounter. As we look at the human side of the
redemptive encounter with God in the Christian community, we
need now to ask, What are the dynamics that move the self to
respond to God with the "Yes," or that hold him back from so
responding? After examining that question we should then ask two
further questions: How are the themes of revelation adapted to
the young? And what are the implications for method in teaching
within the Christian community?

DYNAMICS OF CHANGE

In the most general terms it can be asserted at once that the
dynamic of changes in the self is to be sought in the area of one's
relationships. These are of two chief kinds. One is the interpersonal

relationships, those which one sustains to other selves. The other is the intrapsychic relationships, those which one sustains to himself.

We have to begin by considering interpersonal relationships, because these precede intrapsychic relationships and give shape to them, in the life of the individual. The interpersonal relationships into which the self is born and in which he spends his earliest years are highly dynamic. It is now commonly held that the character structure is formed very early. The present tendency is to assert that it takes its shape during the first four or five years of life, and many would reduce the number of the most formative years much further still.

In these early years formative forces of the greatest importance are at work in the life of the individual long before language can be used as a means of communication. Nonverbal communication thus precedes verbal communication. This is now generally understood in psychology and psychotherapy, and it holds true of course in religion. The fact of nonverbal communication as it concerns the very young has been known in Jewish and in Christian communities from time immemorial.

This means that if revelation is to have any meaning to the very young it must first reach them through nonverbal, nonsymbolical communication. The fact that the grace of God reaches the very youngest may of course be expressed in symbolism through words or through sacramental actions. But unless the symbols participate in the reality for which they stand, the symbols, however hallowed by time and usage, are a mockery.

We know that nonverbal communication is, among other things, the communication of feeling and emotion. The most dynamic nonverbal communication which takes place in the relationships of the early years is the communication of the feeling of acceptance or rejection.

Acceptance and rejection do not have to be verbalized or symbolized in order to be communicated. Acceptance is communicated by such means as looks, the tone of voice, gestures, and actions. So with rejection; it needs no words, no symbols. And when the feeling of rejection is communicated, neither words nor symbols that offer acceptance can overcome the fact of the rejection. The young are not deceived in such matters. They correctly perceive the feeling, whatever the words and symbols. And by the same token, genuine acceptance needs no great protestations of love and concern.

In general, then, the early relationships are the first source of dynamic because they carry the power to form the character structure, and because that character structure constitutes as it were the shape of the channel through which the energies of the self are expressed.

The interpersonal relationships into which the individual is born give him his first feelings toward himself. These early feelings for himself are the first form of his relationship to himself. They begin to set up a relation between the "I" and the "me." They give the first shape to his intrapsychic dynamics. It may be useful to examine the nature of the intrapsychic dynamics further, by means of the concept of tension.

As soon as the self is born, and constantly afterward to a greater or lesser degree, the self is in tension. This tension is a source of dynamic within the self, and in the relationships of the self to other selves, to the world, and to God. Tension in human beings may be thought of as the feeling that things are apart which belong together, and that they will draw still further apart unless something is done to relieve the tension. The tension may be felt as chiefly intrapsychic, or as chiefly interpersonal; but these two cannot be sharply separated, since intrapsychic tension tends to stimulate interpersonal tensions, and vice versa.

As just said, tension may be felt as existing chiefly within the individual self. This is a state of things in one's relations with himself. The tension may be a state of unease because one feels there is a gap of some sort between the way things are within oneself and the way they might be; this is a gap between the actual and the possible. But it is more than merely that. It is a feeling that the gap between the actual and the possible wants to close up. So, for example, one feels tension when he wants to be what he is not, or wants to do what he is not doing, or wants to have feelings which he does not now have, or wants to enjoy some satisfaction which he now misses.

In its more severe form tension gives the feeling that things are in danger of breaking apart within. Common speech abounds in picturesque sayings which attempt to describe this feeling, and people are ingenious in formulating such descriptions. Such expressions as "I feel like I am going to pieces," or "I can't stand much more," are examples. Psychotic forms of speech express the inward state of affairs even more vividly, as when one says he feels as if there were a wire loose inside him.

Tension may exist in one's relationships to other selves. In this situation one's relationship to another individual or to a group carries some kind of threat, or fails to relieve some tension already existing within himself. One's interaction with the other self or selves then expresses his effort to reduce or remove the tension.

Any of the threats to the self which we have previously mentioned tends to produce tension within the self or in one's relationships with others. In previous references to such threats we have usually spoken of them as producing anxiety and concern. Anxiety and concern, however, are not the same as tension. Anxiety and concern, as we have seen, are vague states of apprehensiveness. But the concept of tension points to energy or power which is generated within the self during anxiety or concern. A tension is a system of forces at work, a system in which there is a pull and a counterpull of opposing forces. In a state of tension a system of things, threatened with going still further apart, "wants" to get together again, "pulls" to get together again into repose. If there were no tension at all, each part in the system could go its own way in disregard of the others. But as long as there is tension there is the pull to hold together.

So tension really means that a force is being generated to counteract the threat and relieve the anxiety. This force becomes a "motive" when it can be directed into specific channels. It is for reasons of this kind that we can speak of tension as being a source of dynamic within the self and in one's relations with other selves.

It is unfortunate if the concept of tension becomes associated merely or chiefly with unhealthful conditions of human existence.

It does denote that there is strain, to be sure. But it equally denotes that such and such a state of things, being felt as a threat, arouses the self to want to change that state of things within himself, or in his relations with other persons, or in the world about him. *A state of tension in the human being, then, is a condition in which some capacity in the self is seeking a goal on which it can expend some or even all of its energy.*

Evidences of tension are only too apparent in modern life. Here we can call attention only to four of the forms which tension takes. One is complacency. In complacency there seems at first sight to be no tension at all, but only a desire to be let alone. On closer knowledge of the dynamics of the complacent self, however, it often turns out that this tightness against being disturbed is itself a form of tension. There is a neat balancing off of deeper tensions against one another. One would rather live with the ills which he can manage after a fashion, than to risk opening up a Pandora's box of new ones.

Tension may be felt as discontent. In discontent one knows there is a gap between the actual and the possible, but one does not grasp the true nature of the gap; he asks whether it is in the system of things in the world at large, or in his relationships with others, or just possibly within himself. In discontent one frets, tries many expedients, flounders, and is burdened with resentment. If discontent can only be projected onto other persons, or onto institutions, or onto forces outside oneself, the self can avoid self-understanding and can blame or attack the external enemy. Hence discontent is an opening into possible changes in the self, but it is far more comfortable to make it the ground for trying to change other persons or something in the surrounding world.

Tension may be partly relieved by setting up new, substitute tensions. These substitutes then divert the pressure of the deeper tensions when no creative way of handling the deeper tensions can be found. An individual, a group, a church, or even still greater units in society may in this event be devoted to relieving the substitute tension. Thus, to take but one example, if a religious group finds life in the present world too much for it, that group may retreat to the past and attempt to set up a religious society which exactly duplicates one that existed long ago; or it may retreat into the future by denying the present while it awaits the coming in of the kingdom of God.

Tension may, however, be of a truly creative kind. It can yield an inward dynamic which leads neither to complacency nor to discontent nor to the setting up of substitute tensions. Instead of any of these it may lead to changes in the self of such a kind that the gap between the actual and the possible within the self begins to close up. The self moves toward some goal which is neither a projection of its own discontent nor a substitute to cover failure. In a word, it may move toward profounder selfhood in a spiritual dimension. Thus tension within the self *may* yield the dynamic for changes in the depths of the self.

DYNAMICS OF INTERACTION

The way in which the dynamic arising from intrapsychic tension is handled is profoundly influenced by one's interpersonal relationships. The self, of course, is not in isolation, but is in interaction with other selves. This was true as one began life in infancy, and it continues to be so as the years pass and as one widens his circle. In such interaction both intrapsychic and interpersonal dynamics are drawn into functioning. This interaction is simply the give and take of ordinary life.

Here, however, we are chiefly concerned with the interaction that goes on in the Christian community, with the dynamics of that interaction, and with the resulting changes in persons. Accordingly, attention is now drawn to certain significant aspects of the dynamics of interaction in the Christian community.

One of these we may call the significance of the personal motif. In human interaction the character structure of each person has some stimulus value for each other person with whom one interacts. He has this stimulus value, this way of affecting other persons, because of his own motif.

The term "motif" is here used to denote the self's typical way of responding to other selves as he encounters them. Each character structure ultimately is immensely complex, and highly particularistic for each person. Nevertheless as one begins to move out into relationships with other persons he tends to respond to others and to interact with them in some fairly uniform way. This fairly uniform way of responding to many different persons and in many different situations is his motif.

The personal motif supplies a dynamic factor in the interaction of selves, because each motif represents the movement of a self in relation to other selves. What this means can be better seen if a few common motifs are mentioned as examples.

There is for instance the outgoing self. This person is able to relate readily to others. He is able to affirm other selves, so that they not only feel accepted, but feel stronger when they are in interaction with an outgoing self. He is able to draw forth other selves, and is able to enter into other selves. His anxiety seems to be wholly within normal limits, and his tensions seem to be of a creative kind.

There is the passive dependent self. In his relationships he is rather inert. He depends upon others to do for him, and seems not to be capable of forthgoing. There is the withdrawing self. He is not merely passive, but manages to retreat back into himself when encountering other selves.

There is the aggressive self. He protects himself by making others feel uncomfortable. He puts other persons on the defensive, often accomplishing this in the first remarks in an exchange of conversation. He may attack other persons directly, by making a charge, denying a statement by a flat contradiction, and the like. He may attack other persons indirectly, as by belittling something which they value highly. He is adept at undermining another's position, and seems able to put his finger immediately on another person's weak spot.

There is the affect-hungry self. His need for affection and support is so great that it seems never to be satisfied. He needs forever to be propped up emotionally. He responds to another person by instantly seeking approval and affection. This he may do by some form of action on behalf of the other, or quite as likely by some display of his own suffering so as to win sympathy. He is given to fastening himself onto another. Unable to be an emotional giver himself, he lives emotionally off of others but drains them in so doing.

There is the overconscientious self. He holds up for himself an impossible ideal, and gets much satisfaction from the fact that his ideals are so far above those of "the herd," as he is likely to call them. Or his conscientiousness may take the form of scruples which keep him from acting, or keep him preoccupied with ethical trifles. He may torture himself over some small mistake. He may agonize over his own sin, and yet be unable to accept forgiveness. These examples may serve to illustrate the point that the motif is a dynamic factor in interaction, because each self tends to release his own typical response when encountering other selves.

Another significant aspect of the dynamics of interaction is selective perception. We have repeatedly seen that perception is of the greatest importance in the religious life. This is true for two reasons especially. The first is that God's disclosure of himself to man must be perceived by each human creature before it is revelation to *him*. The other is that one must be able to perceive the meaning of what is transpiring in human relationships in which he participates, otherwise he goes on forever repeating his old motif and nothing new breaks through to him from other selves.

The term "selective perception" denotes the fact that the self has its own pattern of perception, just as one has his own motif in responding to other persons. The self perceives, that is, recognizes meaning in, what is presented from the outer world in light of the meaning which life already has for that self in its own inner world. For example, one can respond positively to those materials of the outer world which fit into his own inner world, giving support and strength to that inner world; and one is likely to respond negatively to the materials of the outer world which threaten his own inner world, or to those which bore him because he sees no connection with his own inner world.

Each person brings his own inner world with him when he comes into a gathering. Thus there is a great diversity of inner worlds in any group of persons. Of each person in a group it must be said that it is *his* inner world which determines the selectivity of his perception and response. And some persons, because of dynamic intrapsychic or interpersonal factors then operating, may come into a group but armor themselves against the group and whatever is going to happen within it.

This kind of perception may be called armored perception. In this case one is trying to protect himself against having his pattern of selective perception disturbed. It is as if he said, "I dare you to get inside *me* with anything *you* can say." Some examples of armored perception are open and obvious in such ways as whispering while someone is trying to address the group, disturbing others, reading irrelevant matter, fidgeting, sleeping. Armored perception is less obvious but no less real in daydreaming, or pursuing a private train of thought. It is quite apparent that in armored perception one is walling himself off from emotional and mental participation.

A third significant aspect of the dynamics of interaction lies in the fact that interaction can lead to a change of personal motif and a change in the pattern of selective perception. We have seen that both the motif and selective perception are dynamic, but that they tend to perpetuate themselves. When persons interact in true two-way communication, however, the pattern of perception can change without a feeling that the self is in danger; and so can the personal motif. The results of interaction can then be changes in persons.

Previously we pointed to several phases of the dynamics of interaction which should now be brought together in this connection, so that no one of these processes may seem to stand off to itself in isolation. We spoke of the two-way process of educing and imparting, where each self leads out the other and at the same time each self imparts itself to the other.

We spoke of interaction at the deeper levels as becoming inter-penetration. In interpenetration the giving self gives itself into another, so that one self as it were enters into another self and becomes part of it. And in interpenetration the receiving self takes into itself another self, in a process called introjection. Thereafter one is hardly able to distinguish where the dynamic effect of the introjected self begins and where it ends.

And we spoke of two-way communication, in which meaning

coming forth out of the deeper reaches of the self can pass back and forth in the dialogue of deepening self-disclosure. It must be obvious that each of these, eduction and impartation, interpenetration and communication, is but a term for some phase of interaction; and that as these go on, changes in the self are taking place.

Still another significant aspect of the dynamics of interaction is the fact that interaction can be either spiritual or demonic. This is true whether we think of interaction as eduction and impartation of selves, or as interpenetration, or as communication. The possibility that interaction in the Christian community can be demonic has to be borne in mind always; else the church begins to make itself into an idol to be worshiped, begins to regard what it communicates as infallible, and withdraws itself from standing under judgment. In such a case the church begins to become a monster, the more terrifying because it claims the name of Christ and offers the grace of God to broken lives.

Interaction can be called demonic when the changes it produces in persons are such as to weaken, damage, paralyze, or delude the self in whom the changes take place. Demonic interaction might lead to such results as these, for example. It might still further solidify a character structure whose motif or whose capacity for perception keeps that self from moving into deeper levels of relationship with men or God. It might result in introjecting one self into another self in such a way that the latter or weaker self is inwardly bound by some stronger self and cannot release himself.

Interaction of a demonic kind may bind the conscience to courses of action which are hurtful to physical or mental health. It may release expressions of hostility in an uncontrolled situation, so that no healing takes place as a result of the discharge of hostility, but only further damage. This is combat and destruction in interaction. It can take place in church quarrels, in the struggle between factions, in schisms, and in religious wars.

Interaction can be called spiritual when the changes it produces in persons are such as to lead the self into a deepening fellowship with God, into fellowship with others in the life of faith, and into fuller realization of its potentialities as a human creature made in the image of God. To put it more compactly, interaction is spiritual when it assists human selves to become what they were created to be.

Interaction which is spiritual in nature can be described in terms of motif and perception. Thus interaction which is spiritual in nature tends to change the motif, releasing the self into the outgoing affirmation of the well-being of others. This is the transmuting of love from love that is self-seeking and self-serving, to love which is self-giving and other-affirming. And it assists the self to perceive new and deeper meanings in what is already familiar, or to perceive some meaning in that which hitherto had no meaning. This is opening the eyes of faith. It is symbolized in Peter's confession of Jesus as the Christ, and in the beholding of the transfiguration.

The most significant of all the aspects of the dynamics of interaction in the Christian community is confrontation itself. The Christian community is confronted by the living God. Faith perceives this living God as standing against whatever is demonic in itself or in its members. And by faith the Christian community perceives the living God as moving toward and into the *koinonia* with redemption from the old life and with power for the new life.

Confrontation means that God is going forth into the *koinonia* of the Christian community, imparting himself into it through creation, lordship, vocation, judgment, redemption, re-creation, providence, and the life of faith. It means that he is seeking to lead out the human selves of the community into deeper responsiveness to himself and to their fellows.

All this means that God is seeking to interpenetrate Spiritually into the human selves and into their interaction in the Christian community, by means of his own disclosure of himself. This is the higher dynamic, the *dunamis* or power of the Spirit. The dynamics of change in the self and the dynamics of interaction become Spiritual when the people in the *koinonia* are open and responsive to this divine dynamic which comes forth from an abyss of love and of power. In fellowship God imparts himself to his people as he leads them forth along the uncharted way.

ADAPTATION OF THEMES

How, then, are the materials of the curriculum related to these dynamic processes of tension, interaction, and change, such as we have been considering? Some general statements will serve to suggest the direction in which the answers may be sought, and will give a setting in which to take up the more specific question of how the themes of revelation are adapted to the young.

The *content* of learning consists of the changes which have taken place in persons as a result of tension, interaction, and the rest of the dynamic processes we have been considering. In the deepest sense of learning, they have "learned" what they have become. From the education point of view this means that we must both broaden and deepen our concept of learning. This is exactly what is taking place in educational psychology.

From the theological point of view it means that we need not be so concerned as once we were to maintain a sharp distinction between act and process in the life of the Christian community. When that was done, some tended to think of all processes as being only "natural," and not "Spiritual." They then tended to think of the Spirit as present in act, but not in process. But it can now be seen more clearly that the important distinction is not between act and process; rather, it is the distinction between spiritual and demonic. A process can be either Spiritual or demonic, depending on the nature of the changes it produces. So too an act can be either, as when an act of decision changes the course of a life, the direction of the change depending on the nature of the response. Each response of "Yes" or "No" is an act of decision. Thus the difference between act and process fades away as the difference between Spiritual and demonic grows clearer.

The *materials* of learning are matters originally outside the self, presented to the self, and employed by responsible persons as means to ends. The ends for which the materials are employed are changes in persons.

There are materials of learning, of course, which are presented to the self in the unguided living which goes on outside any planned educational system. Often the learning that takes places under these conditions is of the greatest importance to the individual. We do not minimize its significance, but here we must restrict consideration to those materials which are used by responsible persons under circumstances where guidance of the changes taking place in persons is possible.

The materials of learning may be presented by life itself in the course of living; or they may be selected and presented according to plans prepared in advance. In either case the materials are potential means to ends, to be used by responsible persons, the leaders, who participate in and guide the changes taking place.

In current literature it is often said that material and method are but two aspects of one and the same thing, and should not be separated. Such a statement holds true only when education is based on a pragmatic philosophy such as that of John Dewey. In that case material and method are said to be two sides of the same process, the process of thinking or problem solving. But education can be based on a philosophy of encounter, and when this is done it will have to take account of confrontation in a way which pragmatism cannot do.

As far as the materials of learning are concerned, taking account of confrontation means that we do not understand learning to be merely or even chiefly a matter of searching for truth. For there is a sense in which truth faces us, presents itself to us, and does so whether we ask for it or not, whether we feel the need for it or not. This is so in all learning and in all education, and is in no way restricted to learning in religion.

But it is of especial significance in Christian education. For when once this is understood, we are set free from the nightmare of trying to permit a curriculum to grow up entirely out of the questions which children are now asking and the needs they now feel. We can with a good educational conscience let the young be confronted in the school, as they are outside the school, by that which will draw forth the deeper questions they are not now asking.

As just observed there are materials which are not planned for but which are presented by life itself. These can be accepted as something that has confronted us, and can be made into materials of learning. For example, there may be some event which occurs in a group while its members are together, stirring up new and deeper questions. Or during the preceding days some event may have befallen some person in the group, such as an accident or death, bringing all the group to face questions of ultimate meaning in life. Or still again some one of the grim threats that overshadow our world may have aroused fresh fears, as when the young hear a wave of conversation about H-bombs, and germ warfare. Instances of the materials which life presents apart from our planning could be given *ad infinitum*.

These materials, presented by life itself, are as it were thrown into an already dynamic situation, precipitating fresh interaction between the persons concerned. All that has been said regarding tension and interaction applies here. The motifs of the selves who are involved, their ability to perceive meaning, the spiritual or demonic nature of the interaction, and the nature of the symbols with which they communicate with one another—all these are relevant to the question of the responses which will be made, and the changes in selves which will take place. These changes *are* the content of the learning.

And there are the materials of learning which are planned for, and introduced purposefully as means to ends. These are the materials selected by the writer of curriculum materials, by the teacher planning for a unit or a session, directors, and any others who plan the use of the materials of learning. Here there is an immense range of materials to draw upon. Biography, history, music and art of all kinds, poetry, drama, and literature of all kinds, projected materials, materials recorded for the reproduction of sound, broadcasts and televised materials—all these and many more make up an embarrassment of riches.

In what follows, however, we concentrate the thought upon the materials of learning which are, or may be, drawn from the Bible. It will be apparent that we do not assume a completely planned curriculum to be the only permissible curriculum. Quite the contrary is true; for we assume that the dialogue of true two-way communication can never be anticipated in full. It will be observed also that we do not assume the materials of learning which are drawn from the Bible to be the only materials of learning appropriate to a planned curriculum of Christian education. On the contrary, we assume there is a legitimate place for any or all such materials as have just been mentioned; namely, biography and the rest.

But in this book we are especially concerned with the relation between education and revelation. We have considered the themes of the Bible as being persistent aspects of revelation, directed toward human predicament. And now we should follow through by asking how the themes are adapted to the young. This we shall attempt to do by affirming certain propositions having to do with the selection and adaptation of Biblical materials. These propositions follow.

1. The nature of the Bible itself gives us our first great clue as to its use with the young. The Bible contains a record of revelation. In the Biblical understanding of revelation, revelation commonly is a disclosure to those who are in mature years. Through them it is to reach the young of the religious community.

Accordingly the Bible, as a record of revelation, is chiefly taken up with the affairs and the reflections of persons in adult life. This is why it is so difficult to find Biblical passages which can be used, just as they stand, with children in the first few years of life. This does not mean that the children have been forgotten. Quite the opposite is true. There is abundant evidence that they were the object of warm affection and deep concern. But with the exception of a few passages the Bible is not *addressed* to children. Overwhelmingly it is addressed to adults, and to a lesser degree to youth.

What then is to be done with the Bible in teaching children, especially younger children, in the Christian community? The problem thus presented to the Christian community is really in the nature of a predicament. The church has faced it from the beginning, and there is no neat solution which can be easily followed. Two contrasted solutions have tempted the church in recent times. One is the apparently simple solution of postponing the use of Biblical materials until some specified age. The other is a scissors-and-paste method of garnering and classifying all the materials which it is supposed a child of a given age can understand, and presenting these. It was only when the poverty of both these solutions began to be apparent that the magnitude of the predicament began to be evident again in modern time.

What we have been proposing is that we should let the nature of revelation itself govern us in our use of the record of revelation. If the materials of the Bible are to be used in keeping with the nature of the revelation which they record, we must learn to think of communication as the Bible thinks of communication. This means we can learn to think of that which can be communicated through relationships, as being prior to that which can be communicated through words and symbols.

This means also that in the strategy of education planning, we need to begin with the adults. When there are changes in the adults of a Christian community and in their relationships with one another, the young of the community are entering into a changing system of dynamic interaction before they even come together in the church. One denomination which has taken seriously the principle of beginning with the adults seems at present to be entering into a remarkable renaissance of Christian education.

2. The principal purpose of using the Bible in the Christian community is the purpose of the continuing encounter. This we have already affirmed previously. Here it is to be seen as governing the choice of materials from the Bible, and the purpose in using them. The concept of themes offers one way of keeping this central purpose in view, and facilitating the selection of materials which may be used as means for the accomplishment of that purpose.

In the concept of themes the materials of the Bible are used as a means of precipitating man's encounter with God, who continues to confront us in creation, in lordship, in vocation, in judgment, in redemption, in re-creation, in providence, and in the life of faith. Furthermore, the concept of themes offers a way of drawing freely upon the Old Testament and yet keeping its materials always oriented by the New Testament, so that the God who is encountered in the Christian community may be perceived as the God and Father of our Lord Jesus Christ.

3. In revealing himself to man, God has freely used what are now often called nonverbal means of communication. The record

of revelation has to be a verbal record, but what is recorded is often a Self-impartation which is not verbal, but is nonverbal communication. Hence the themes of revelation lend themselves to communication from person to person in nonverbal ways.

This means that the essence of what God has imparted to man by revelation can be communicated to the very young before they are old enough to understand words, indeed, from the beginning of life. The essence of God's Self-impartation is love, the *agape* of which the New Testament speaks when it is said that God is love. Man, receiving this Self-giving love, can never express it perfectly in his relationships with others, but he *can* express it, even if imperfectly.

The love which is *agape* can be communicated to the very young in the *koinonia* of the Christian family and church. This means that the essence of the revelation which the Bible records can begin to reach the very young before they can understand one word of speech. As Paul Tillich has shown, this love, *agape,* is itself creative and is the true ground of Christian education.[1]

4. In revelation, God has communicated with man by means of "the word." But this does not mean that God's speech with man is a verbalistic transaction, as when one man utters spoken words that strike the ears of another man. Biblically, whatever is uttered in communication is a "word." The "word" may, for example, be a subjective experience of encounter which is perceived *as* encounter; it may be an event in the surrounding world; or it may be a person. God's most revealing "word" to man was a Person who was called the Logos, the Word.

We for our part in using the Bible for the purpose of the continuing encounter are not tied to the exact words of the Bible as the only way of communicating the message which those words contain. The Bible itself shows that the highest form of communication is not by means of precise verbalism, but is carried on by means of what passes between persons in personal encounter.

Hence we do not need to feel delinquent in the Christian community if we do not use the exact language of the Bible when we use the materials of the Bible with children. When the Bible utters something that is relevant to children, the language in which it is uttered can be adapted to the speech which children use.

5. The theological meaning of the themes can be communicated by adapting the terms used to the age and stage of development of the persons concerned. This holds true not only for children, but for immature youth and adults as well. The Bible lends itself remarkably well to this kind of adaptation, because so much of what it records in connection with each great theme is not abstract, not general, but highly specific as in the case of the event or the person.

Two pieces of work in recent time are very suggestive in connection with the adaptation of theological meaning. Ross Snyder, writing after experimentation with children of three and four years of age, is convinced that the essence of many of the great doctrines of Christian faith is experienced by children in a good nursery school, and the doctrines to which he refers are not unlike what we have called themes in this book.[2]

Randolph Crump Miller has illustrated the adaptation of theological meaning to the various age groups in the church.[3] What he describes is not the making of a catechism to be used as a vehicle for one-way communication. Rather it is a two-way communication in which the meaning of the symbols is developed in the dialogue going on between the interacting selves.

6. There are subsidiary purposes, as well as a principal purpose, in using the Bible in the Christian community. One of the subsidiary purposes, as already affirmed, is that of remembrance and appropriation. When this purpose is pursued, it means that the materials of the Bible are used in such a way that the people of today become familiar with the history of the people of God as it is told in the Bible.

The purpose of remembrance and appropriation is fulfilled, at least in part, by three classes of material drawn from the Bible. One is the principal events in the history which is related in the Bible. A second is the great stories of the Bible. A third is the principal characters who are known through the Bible. To a considerate extent these classifications overlap, but between them they contain a treasure in which every child in the Christian community has the right to participate. Standing in its own worth as something which it is good to know, remember, and make one's own, the history is told to the young for no ulterior purpose beyond the purpose of remembrance and appropriation. But when it is known and appropriated it provides a foundation of specifics which underlie the great theological meanings of the themes of revelation.

7. Since the revelation of God and the predicaments of man are in correspondence, the materials drawn from the Bible to be used in the Christian community should be chosen with the anxiety and the predicaments of the people of our own time in view. To do this is to serve a second contributory purpose in using the Bible mentioned previously; namely, to search for the relevance of revelation.

There is a hunger at this point which already exists in a great number of persons. Coming into a more mature outlook on life, asking the great questions which men in all times have asked, perhaps sobered and even bewildered by the signs of our own times, they would like to know whether the Bible has any word to speak to their condition. Not a few make some attempt to read the Bible for themselves, but give up without knowing how to find a thread they can follow, and not knowing what to make out of much that they find.

When it is remembered that each theme speaks to man in predicament, one who plans a responsible use of the Bible is kept back from getting lost in antiquarian trifles. He is held back from pedantry if he has learning, and from false modesty if he lacks learning. For in seriousness he is asking the ancient question, "What *saith* the Scripture?"

This does not mean, however, that we must always have a specific "problem" in view whenever a portion of Biblical material is selected. When man is confronted by the living God something will be said *to him*, and often enough it will have nothing to do with the question which he brought with him into the encounter. It may be a wholly new question which he for his part must now answer.

To forget this, and to try to confine the use of the Bible to "problem-centered" teaching, is to forget the nature of revelation and the nature of its record. In this event the Bible is reduced to the level of utility and is asked to justify itself before public opinion in a practical-minded Western culture. It is no longer a spokesman for the living God, facing our day with judgment and with mercy. If its use can be justified only on the ground of some educational theory, it can no longer be heard as the word of the Lord of life. Instead, it has become an insignificant little idol. And like the Baal of Elijah's time, it will be silent to our entreaty.

8. It is not necessary that every portion of material should be chosen with the purpose of securing a specific outcome in conduct. Nor is it necessary that every portion of Biblical material used should be turned in the direction of a "conduct outcome." If the material is used primarily for the purpose of preparing the way for the encounter with God, we must trust the relationship with God which is established, or renewed, or deepened within the encounter; and are not obliged to be constantly urging our own notions of what should come out of the encounter.

To fasten attention on the specifics of conduct, and to measure success in teaching by the extent to which these specific outcomes have been achieved, is to encourage a relapse. Religiously it is a relapse from Christianity toward orthodox Judaism. This is so because it tends to forget the liberty of the Christian, and begins to prescribe the details of daily life, much as the rabbis did when they began to create the unwritten law contained in the Mishnah. Psychologically it is a relapse toward behaviorism, with its theories of learning which overlooked the existence of the self.

The question which we ultimately face here is really a double question, having to do with the nature of faith: What is the Christian understanding of the nature of the faith which transforms life, and what is the nature of the educator's own faith as he lives and works with people? To put the issue in New Testament terms: Is he called upon to have *faith in faith* as that which transforms life, or is he called to have *faith in works* which will bring one into favor with God and man? Each of these produces its own kind of eduction, or leading out of people. The latter educational faith means basically that the educator is leading people into moralism. The former means that basically he is leading them toward faith.

9. In selecting materials from the Bible there should be pro-

gression in the development of a theme from one age group to another. The young then are less likely to be wearied by overuse of the same materials, and more likely to have a sense of advancing in their journey into the Bible. Progression is possible in many respects. For example, there can be a movement from the more simple to the more complex in all sorts of materials, as age advances.

Progression in the use of symbols is possible also. From symbols that are concrete and highly specific, there can be advancement toward those that are more general, and more difficult to grasp. The lists of symbols presented in Chapter VI will illustrate such a progression, beginning with the highly specific. Presenting Biblical materials which employ Biblical symbols serves still another contributory purpose mentioned earlier, that is, gaining acquaintance with Biblical symbols as a means of communication in the Christian community.

New and fresh ways of drawing upon the symbols of the Bible as materials of learning can be developed by the exercise of ordinary ingenuity. This is a rich field for exploration, especially in a prosaic age when so much that is bottled up cannot be expressed in prosaic terms. The place of symbols in the teaching of children will probably have to be reexamined in the light of clinical experience, where children often can begin a two-way communication only by the use of symbols which they spontaneously produce. Such speech, of course, is exactly what a large part of the Bible is: the spontaneous but symbolical call of the troubled soul. And as for persons past childhood, there needs to be progression in their acquaintance with Biblical symbols. Otherwise, large sections of the Bible remain unknown territory to some, and an unhealthy refuge for others.

10. Each theme of revelation probably is relevant ultimately to every age in the life span. But some are obviously more relevant than others to the young, while other themes are more relevant to the more mature than to the very young. For example, the theme of vocation is appropriate to the very youngest, because it has to do with the meaning of the Christian community, with being drawn into it and accepted by it. This can be communicated non-

verbally from the earliest days of life, and it can be communicated verbally and symbolically as age advances.

11. The use of themes as a basis of curriculum planning needs to be carried out on an experimental basis. On theological, philosophical, and psychological grounds we can arrive at statements of principle. A soundly constructed basis which contains all these elements has been sorely needed, to underlie the planning of curriculum in general and the use of Biblical materials in particular. But when such a basis is constructed we are in no way relieved of the need to put the results of such thinking to a critical test in experimental use.

To do this is but to carry the principle of encounter on to its logical conclusion. Those who are more mature participate with others in the Christian community in the encounter with God. Participating in the encounter they participate in the changes that take place in the encounter. This is adult learning; it is also growth in grace.

PRINCIPLES OF METHOD

When it is understood that Christian education takes place in the Christian community and within the encounter, that its process is the process of interaction between persons, that its dynamic arises in one's relation to himself and others, and that its concern is that human selves may enter into the high destiny for which they were created—when such foundations are established what is to be said concerning method in Christian education?

It should be urged at once that the primary question is not whether some one method is superior to all others, and principally to be relied upon in Christian education. Rather the question is of this kind: When *any* method is proposed or used, how do we decide whether or not it is appropriate to Christian education?

The core of concern in any method and with any materials is communication. This does not mean the communication of materials which are outside the self, with the purpose of getting them into the self. It means two-way communication between selves. The first test of method is, Does it facilitate two-way communication between selves? If it does, it is an effective method. But we still do not know whether it is a spiritual or a demonic method, as used. Hence the second test is, What is the nature of the interaction which it sets up between persons? If it facilitates spiritual interaction, then religiously viewed it is a good method. If it facilitates demonic interaction, it is an unsound method when viewed on any grounds, because it proves damaging to selves.

The implications of such a statement can be better seen by taking observations of this principle from several points of view.

No one method can be relied upon to produce a spiritually dynamic situation by all who use it, even if they follow directions never so faithfully. The history of Christian education is full of instances of idolatrous respect for any method one may mention. That method, whatever it may be, has been associated sometimes with spiritual changes, and sometimes with demonic changes, in persons. Hence one is put on guard against adopting some particular method as *the* method for Christian education. Equally, one is put on guard against fleeing from one fad to another in educational method in search of an educational city of refuge where he can dwell in safety with no haunting fear of failure to pursue him.

Any method seems to hold within itself at least some possibility of being a demonic instrument if the personal motif of the parent, teacher, leader, or minster is not itself spiritual in nature; or if such a person is not able to perceive the meaning of the interaction taking place, or the relation of his material to that interaction.

Any method seems to hold at least some possibility of being a spiritual instrument if the one using it has a personal motif which is spiritual in nature, and is able to perceive the meaning of the interaction taking place and the relation of his material to that interaction. Thus if we reckon teachers as great when they have participated in deep changes in selves for which their students remain grateful, we shall find that great teachers have used a range of method so wide as to be quite embarrassing to the educational theorist.[4]

Any method holds the possibility of being a demonic instrument if it permits any person to remain detached and in a position where he can try to manipulate his child, his students, the officers of a church, or a congregation as if they were objects to be done to, whether in the name of scientific research or of religious fervor.

Any method holds at least some promise of being a spiritual instrument if it permits the individual who is responsible for using it to become personally involved in a situation where spiritual, and not demonic, interaction can take place.

When we were considering the materials of learning we gave especial attention to Biblical materials; similarly here we may give especial attention to method in using the Biblical materials. If the core of concern in the use of any method and any material is communication between selves, this continues to be true when it comes to the method of using Biblical material in the church. We do not have to develop special methods of using the Bible, different from methods used with other materials, *provided the center of concern in all material and in all methods continues to be communication between selves.* For in this event method is simply the means employed to facilitate the encounter between selves in two-way communication, and to clear the way for the continuing encounter with God.

It is possible to identify certain principles which apply to method in using the Bible. These principles do not in themselves determine which methods to use. They do, however, offer bases on which various methods of using Biblical materials can be weighed. And each of them offers a statement of some aspect of communication between selves which is needed in teaching, and which imaginative insight can find ways to realize. Each of them is based on some fact in the psychology of interaction.

The principle of nonverbal communication. Since the earliest communication in which the self participates is nonverbal, and since at all ages nonverbal communication is a channel for two-way communication of feeling and emotion, this form of communication must be taken into account in using Biblical materials as well as all other materials. The essence of the revelation which the Bible records, which is love, depends primarily upon nonverbal means for its communication and for its validation. This holds true for all ages in the life span, from the youngest to the oldest.

When it comes to the formal use of Biblical materials, the nonverbal undertones and overtones which accompany the use of the material in teaching are powerful factors in the interaction between selves. For example, the emotional overtones surrounding the use of Biblical passages communicate the leader's yearning for reconciliation, or perhaps on the contrary his rejection of persons. A vast charge of hostility can be expressed in the mere reading of a few verses; and, by the same token, so can a great compassion. The same material used by a leader in one mood may constitute an invitation to explore the Bible, while used in another mood it may become a lash with which the listener is publicly scourged.

The principle of participation. If it is accepted that the chief purpose in using the Bible in the Christian community is that of preparing the way for the continuing encounter, methods will be sought which help people of today to stand inside the Bible and participate with its people in their encounter with God. This means, for example, seeing what was seen then, hearing what was heard, and feeling what was felt.

In the case of a story or an event, it means participating with the people who took part in it then. In the case of a belief it means standing beside those who held it, to understand why they did, and what this conviction meant to them in their life of faith. In the case of a confrontation it means standing beside them in their predicament, and with them feeling the strength of the "Yes" or the "No" with which they made their answer.

As such movements within the self take place, we participate in the Bible. We move across the gulf of distance and otherness, and stand beside its people on the stage where they stood. We participate with them in the joys and sorrows, the defeats and the victories, through which they passed as again and again they were met by the living God. In any such use of the Bible, the Bible becomes part of the living environment that surrounds the self in the Christian community.

The principle of identification. Given the opportunity for genuine participation in the Bible, we can expect to find some degree of identification taking place. If we stand beside its people and participate with them, they are no longer mere objects to be "objectively studied." By participating, we ourselves become involved.

These are people whom we know. We could have made exactly the same mistakes, committed the same sins; it may well enough be true that we have. We are exposed to our own gaze, standing there so long ago. It is with us as it was with a young woman who came into an office one day, carrying a new biography of Hitler. Slamming it on a desk she said tensely, "That's me."

With whom will the identification take place? In using Biblical materials with a group it is quite likely there will be emotional identification with the "bad" character, as well as with the "good" man or woman. Such identification need not cause dismay. It permits one to recognize openly the nature of his own conflict, and it helps the leader to understand the character structure of persons in his own group. We are dealing here with the demonic element which is in every character. When it is censored out of the material, what is left is goody-goody dullness.

There is another kind of identification, and that is standing beside those who entered the lists where the issues were matters of life and death. These are the people who chose life, and in the end won. But these are not the saints of the plaster bust, the halo, and the sickly chromo. As Reinhold Niebuhr is fond of saying, the saints of the Bible really are a seedy lot. And this of course is the reason why we can be at home with them, and they with us. They are being made whole in the hand of God, yes. But they never cease to be very, very human.

The relation of the believer to Jesus Christ, in one of its aspects, is identification. This does not mean that one is to consider himself to be a "little Christ," as some in modern times would have it. It means that in faith we stand beside him in his death and resurrection in such a way that his death becomes our death to an old self, and his resurrection our rising again to become a new self. As one means to such ends, materials dealing with the life of Jesus will be so used as to keep his life real to those who have not yet come to know him. If then he should become transfigured before their eyes, so that Jesus is perceived to be the Christ, the genuine manhood which is in his Sonship need not be lost.

The principle of perception. To a large extent the human response to revelation consists in the perception of meaning, or the failure to perceive meaning, in that which confronts the self. Biblical material is a means for changing the perception of the meaning in the total configuration of things which life presents. When a change in perception occurs, the meaning in life has to that degree been transformed.

Much that is recorded in the Bible deals with just such transformations of meaning. The transformation is often expressed in symbolical terms such as hearing a voice which gives a command, seeing a vision, and recovering from blindness. Comparable experiences from that time until now have accompanied profound changes in the meaning of life, which have overtaken individuals. And on a lesser scale every new insight, being a new perception, discloses new meaning.

Methods of dealing with all such materials are needed which will dramatize the accounts, not only of lesser disclosures such as come to all men, but also those "impossible" accounts which are among the classics of the record of revelation. These materials deserve the right to tell their own story of newness felt and newness perceived, to each generation. And if the church grows too protective toward the Bible, like the children of a very aged mother who fear what she may say in public, then the people who should have heard these stories in the church will have to get them from stage and screen where miracles of transformed meaning are better understood.

The principle of symbolic communication. Since so much human communication is by means of symbols, and since the symbols of the Bible are the common language of Christendom, methods of teaching will be sought which create at least two kinds of situation. One is the situation in which the leader can recognize and respond to symbolic expression by any member of his group. Wayne E. Oates has pointed out that many persons who are deeply disturbed are trying to communicate by using Biblical symbols, and the symbols which they use are a clue to the nature of their distress.[5] The other is situations in which the significance of symbolic communication regarding human predicament and regarding divine revelation can be explored with full candor and in complete safety.

The principle of ambivalence. The feelings which a human

being entertains toward any one object ordinarily are mixed. Toward one and the same person affection is mingled with rejection, like with dislike, love with hatred. This ambivalence must be allowed for in the life of faith, else impossible demands are placed upon the human creature who is expected to be perfect in love and faith, but in reality cannot be perfect in either.

Methods of using Biblical materials must allow a place for ambivalence in response to the record of revelation. As the self faces the symbols by means of which revelation is communicated, there has to be a place for the "No" of doubt, incredulity, and rejection, as well as for the "Yes" of acknowledgment and submission in response to God. Methods must allow for the resulting dialogue, in which there is no shadow boxing. The "I will not believe" uttered by Thomas is as truly a part of the pilgrimage of faith as is Peter's confession, "Thou art the Christ."

Methods are indicated which encourage interaction between persons in small groups. The small group in interaction has always played a great part in the life of the church, from the band of twelve apostles to the modern cell group. The small group easily falls into a stereotype, as has happened in many churches. But always it holds possibilities of deeper interaction, and small groups intensively interacting commonly appear whenever there is a renaissance of Christian education.

The principle of ultimacy. If the center of concern in all methods is communication, what is to be said of communication itself? Is it a means to some further end, or is it an ultimate good in itself?

That question is a great divide; perhaps so in any time, certainly so in ours. It is the same question which was met earlier in this book: Is the Christian community concerned primarily with one-way communication, or with two-way communication? The communication with which man is now being deluged is the one-way communication of pressure, propaganda, and manipulation. But so far from bridging the distance between men, it only widens the gulf and raises the barriers. On a world scale we call it a cold war, or psychological warfare. And it can go on in the church whenever one person tries to compel the beliefs or the actions of other men.

The communication for which there is now such desperate need in the world is two-way communication. This is the communication which becomes communion. The communion to which true communication leads is an ultimate good. Method which facilitates or produces true communication has in it what religion knows as grace.

Communion, in which persons can open themselves to one another in complete security, is understood in Christianity as an ultimate, an end in itself. Christian faith sets it forth in symbolic terms as God's final gift to man. It is pictured as a state of things in which even the beasts no longer rend one another; and men, no longer sorrowing in separation, nor afraid of one another in their togetherness, dwell eternally in the presence of God. And because such a state of things is utterly beyond all that man now knows, this is to be in the day of the Lord, in the age to come. But it is always to be kept in mind that this is not mere vision. The present realities of the Christian community are an initiation into such communion, in so far as that community is a *koinonia*.

And communion, in which persons can open themselves to one another in complete security—is not this the religious form of the ultimate good which we seek in secular terms whenever we affirm a belief in democracy, or plead for a community of nations in which there shall be peace? The secular vision and the religious vision have a deep kinship. But in the latter it is understood that man, noble as he is in his potentiality, espies an end to which he cannot attain by his own unaided power.

THE POWER TO BECOME

The power to become is both a right and an empowering.

It is the right to become that which we were created to be. But to affirm this right in our own day is to speak to men who carry a sense of lost destiny. The sense of human destiny is so profoundly lost that we are disoriented. We try to remember what that destiny is. On the world scale, is it to dwell in peace or is it to wipe out the other half of the human race? On the personal scale, is it to be a little higher than the other animals or is it to be a little lower than the angels?

In several of the Psalms the expression "my glory" is used, appearing in parallel with "my soul," or "my heart," or simply "I."[6] This shows that "my soul" and "my glory" are interchangeable terms in these Psalms. The human soul, the self, is felt by the singer as noble, having both dignity and splendor.

But why can man so regard himself? It is because glory, which is a mark of selfhood in God, is also a mark of selfhood in man. To be a self is a glory. So the singer, in an hour of ecstasy, can cry out to his own soul, "Awake up, my glory."[7] This is awakening to the right to become. It is claiming the destiny for which a man was born.

But after one begins to know himself for what he is, what then? There must be more than merely a right. The myths of men are full of stories of those whose tragedy was only this: they saw what they might be, but could not possess it. And it is this, is it not, which marks our own age with such unbelievable tragedy: to have caught glowing sight of what we and our world might become, and now——?

The power to become *is* more than a right, more than a vision. It is an empowering. In this, as in the right, man has been given a great gift. But with this, as with the right, he has to claim it. For there is a *dunamis*, "the dynamic which energizes in us."[8] It is within man, yet it is the power of God.

Of the power to become, in this double sense of a right and an empowering, we have tried to speak.

Notes

Chapter I

THE HUMAN SELF

[1] Cf. J. Ruesch and G. Bateson, *Communication, the Social Matrix of Psychiatry* (New York, W. W. Norton & Co., 1951), p. 123.

[2] Cf., for example, such titles as C. G. Jung, *Modern Man in Search of a Soul*, translated by W. S. Dell and C. F. Baynes (New York, Harcourt, Brace & Co., 1934); K. A. Menninger, *Man Against Himself* (New York, Harcourt, Brace & Co., 1938); Erich Fromm, *Man for Himself* (New York, Rinehart & Co., 1947); Rollo May, *Man's Search for Himself* (New York, W. W. Norton & Co., 1953); P. M. Symonds, *The Ego and the Self* (New York, Appleton-Century-Crofts, 1951); A. T. Jersild, *In Search of Self* (New York, Bureau of Publications, Teachers College, Columbia University, 1952).

[3] Genesis 2:7.

[4] Leviticus 17:11, "The *nephesh* of the flesh is in the blood." Cf. also verse 14.

[5] L. J. Sherrill, *Guilt and Redemption* (Richmond, John Knox Press, 1945), Chap. 7 gives particulars.

[6] Romans 8:23.

[7] See especially I Corinthians 15.

[8] See, e.g., II Corinthians 5:1 ff.

[9] Cf. Reinhold Niebuhr, *The Nature and Destiny of Man* (New York, Charles Scribner's Sons, 1941), Vol. I, Chap. 1. The present wide use of the concept of self-transcendence seems to be due largely to Reinhold Niebuhr's introduction of the term. His *The Self and the Dramas of History* (New York, Charles Scribner's Sons, 1955) further develops the concept of self-transcendence and is especially suggestive

in its treatment of the dialogues of the self. However, it was published while this book was in press, hence could not be taken into account in the text of the present work.

[10] See, e.g., R. H. Bonthius, *Christian Paths to Self-Acceptance* (New York, King's Crown Press, 1948).

[11] Cf. J. V. L. Casserley, *The Christian in Philosophy* (New York, Charles Scribner's Sons, 1951), pp. 111, 150 ff., and especially 154.

[12] Otto Rank, *Psychology and the Soul* (Philadelphia, University of Pennsylvania Press, 1950), Chap. 1.

[13] Casserley, *op. cit.*, pp. 151–152, 155. Quoted by permission of the publisher. Cf. also the same author's book *Graceful Reason* (Greenwich, Seabury Press, 1954), Chaps. I and II.

[14] Cf. Paul Tillich, "The Two Types of Philosophy of Religion," *Union Seminary Quarterly Review*, Vol. I, May, 1946.

[15] Compare the account of personal encounter with the God who discloses himself as "I am" in Exodus 3.

[16] This concept is Biblically presented in the account of the creation of man in Genesis 1:26, 27. For a more thorough discussion of the concept of the image of God, and for the two chief points of emphasis which I have developed differently because the context is different, see David E. Roberts, *Psychotherapy and a Christian View of Man* (New York, Charles Scribner's Sons, 1950), Chap. 5.

Chapter II

Threats to the Self

[1] Rollo May, *The Meaning of Anxiety* (New York, The Ronald Press Co., 1950), p. 193. In May's terms "objects" evidently means either other persons, or things outside the self; and the "security base" is a value or values which the individual regards as "essential to his existence as a personality" (p. 191). Quotations used by permission of the publisher.

[2] Paul Tillich, *The Courage to Be* (New Haven, Yale University Press, 1952), Chap. 2.

[3] Cf. R. May, *op. cit.*, Chap. 6, especially pp. 197 ff., where the differences between normal and neurotic anxiety are summarized.

[4] Simone de Beauvoir believes that in the course of normal life men achieve individuality and self-transcendence more readily and more spontaneously than women do. She attributes this to the different psychological effects of the reproductive functions in men as compared

with women. *The Second Sex,* trans. by H. M. Parshley (New York, Alfred A. Knopf, 1952), Chap. 1.

⁵ L. J. Saul, *Emotional Maturity* (New York, J. B. Lippincott Co., 1947), p. 177.

⁶ A. J. Toynbee, *A Study of History,* abridged by D. C. Somervell (New York, Oxford University Press, 1947), Chap. 19.

⁷ For example: K. Horney, *Neurosis and Human Growth* (New York, W. W. Norton & Co., 1950); Fritz Kunkel, *What It Means to Grow Up* (New York, Charles Scribner's Sons, 1936); H. A. Overstreet, *The Mature Mind* (New York, W. W. Norton & Co., 1949); L. J. Saul, *Emotional Maturity* (New York, J. B. Lippincott Co., 1947). The effects of fear in disturbing growth are presented in Bonaro Overstreet, *Understanding Fear in Ourselves and Others* (New York, Harper & Brothers, 1951). Ernest M. Ligon, in *Their Future Is Now* (New York, The Macmillan Co., 1939) and in other works, has insisted that norms for testing the development of Christian personality can be found for the various age levels.

⁸ As, e.g., in C. A. Whitaker and T. P. Malone, *The Roots of Psychotherapy* (New York, The Blakiston Co., 1953).

⁹ K. Horney, *Our Inner Conflicts* (New York, W. W. Norton & Co., 1945), p. 96. Quoted by permission.

¹⁰ Horney, *Neurosis and Human Growth* (New York, W. W. Norton & Co., 1950).

¹¹ Frank West, The Authoritarian Personality (unpublished MS.). Quoted by permission.

¹² The concept of "the real self" is now much used in psychological literature. While it has proved to be a valuable concept for many purposes, it has not been used in this book because of its ambiguity. When the term "the real self" is employed, it often is impossible to know which of several possible meanings is intended. For example, (1) it can legitimately mean ontologically real, i.e., that the self is a real being, and not only a becoming, a process, a phenomenon, etc. But apparently this meaning is not common in the literature, while the ontological reality of the self is central in our treatment. (2) It might, and commonly does, mean the kind of reality which results when one gets rid of his defense mechanisms, his self-deception, his masks, his shams, etc. This important meaning we have incorporated under such terms as falsity in the self, truth in the self, and self-understanding. (3) It might, and apparently does often, mean that the native constitution and endowment of the self is highly particularistic, sets the proper direction

of one's destiny, and needs to be discovered by each individual. This meaning, along with that of the ontological reality of the self, we have incorporated under the term "self-knowledge."

Chapter III

THE CHRISTIAN COMMUNITY

[1] The psychological significance of relationships is, of course, the subject of a large and growing literature, in which the contributions of Harry Stack Sullivan, Otto Rank, and Karen Horney deserve especial recognition. The theological significance of relationships has been suggestively treated in recent time by Reuel Howe in *Man's Need and God's Action* (Greenwich, The Seabury Press, 1953). It happens that I read Howe's work only after the present book had been written, and was startled to observe how many parallels there are in thought and even in expression. Among older works on the theological significance of relationships, Horace Bushnell's *Christian Nurture* is classic, affirming an organic unity between parents and children which is more than physical heredity, and affirming the crucial importance of the pre-language years in a child's life; see, for example, Part II, Chap. I, of the 1888 edition.

[2] G. Florovsky, in *The Universal Church in God's Design* (New York, Harper & Brothers, n.d.), p. 43. Quoted by permission.

[3] *Ibid.*, p. 43. Quoted by permission.

[4] *Ibid.*, p. 44. Quoted by permission.

[5] For a brief summary of the chief opinions regarding the nature of the church, see S. M. Cavert, "The Meaning of Amsterdam, 1948, for the American Churches," in *Yearbook of American Churches, 1949*, ed. G. F. Ketcham, pp. 164–169 (New York, Federal Council of the Churches of Christ in America, 1949). For a sympathetic but frank summary of points of difference between the Roman Church and the Protestant churches, see William Adams Brown, *The Church, Catholic and Protestant* (New York, Charles Scribner's Sons, 1935).

[6] H. S. Commager, *The American Mind* (New Haven, Yale University Press, 1950).

[7] Stringfellow Barr, *The Pilgrimage of Western Man* (New York, Harcourt, Brace & Co., 1949), Chaps. 15, 16.

[8] See, e.g., C. A. Beard and M. R. Beard, *History of the United States*, rev. ed. (New York, The Macmillan Co., 1934), Chap. 24.

[9] The sociological inquiry into the nature and relevance of the

church is well exemplified in the long series of monographs published by the Institute of Social and Religious Research, culminating in a summary volume by H. Paul Douglass and Edmund de S. Brunner, entitled *The Protestant Church as a Social Institution* (New York, Harper & Brothers, 1935).

[10] The inquiry into the relevance of theological education is best represented by the report on the Study of Theological Education published in four volumes under the title *The Education of American Ministers,* by Mark A. May and others (New York, Harper & Brothers, 1934).

[11] The results are summarized in two reports by Oren H. Baker: one in Bulletin 18, American Association of Theological Schools, pp. 141 ff. (June, 1948); the other in Bulletin 19, A.A.T.S., pp. 85 ff. (June, 1950).

[12] Studies of leadership in the church, and especially in the church school, are found, for example, in F. L. Knapp, *Leadership Education in the Church* (New York, Abingdon Press, 1933); Price H. Gwynn, *Leadership Education in the Local Church* (Philadelphia, Westminster Press, 1952); Floy S. Hyde, *Protestant Leadership Education Schools* (New York, Bureau of Publications, Teachers College, Columbia University, 1950). Among the general studies of leadership, with emphasis on personality and interaction, are to be mentioned, e.g., the following: Robert Bales, *Interaction Process Analysis* (Cambridge, Mass., Addison Wesley Press, 1951); Ruth Cunningham et al., *Understanding Group Behavior of Boys and Girls* (New York, Bureau of Publications, Teachers College, Columbia University, 1951).

[13] Frank West, The Authoritarian Personality (unpublished MS.)

Chapter IV

WITHIN THE ENCOUNTER

[1] H. W. Robinson, *Inspiration and Revelation in the Old Testament* (Oxford, Clarendon Press, 1946), Chap. 22.

[2] *Ibid.,* Chap. 1.

[3] William Temple, *Nature, Man and God* (London, Macmillan & Co., 1934), p. 486. Quoted by permission.

[4] Hebrews 4:13.

[5] Temple, *op. cit.,* Chap. 12, especially pp. 315 ff.

[6] Richard Niebuhr, *The Meaning of Revelation* (New York, The Macmillan Co., 1941), pp. 109–110. Quoted by permission.

7 Colossians 2:9.

8 John 14:9.

9 John 1:1–14.

10 John 1:17. Cf. E. Brunner, *The Divine-Human Encounter* (Philadelphia, Westminster Press, 1943), Chap. 5.

11 John 18:38.

12 John 1:12.

13 John 8:32; 14:6.

14 II Corinthians 5:19.

15 Revelation 21:5.

16 The work of Paul H. Vieth, reported in *Objectives in Religious Education* (New York, Harper & Brothers, 1930), was a landmark in defining the ends sought in Christian education. Since his study, programs in the denominations have been deeply influenced by his findings.

17 J. Ruesch and G. Bateson, *Communication, the Social Matrix of Psychiatry* (New York, W. W. Norton & Co., 1951), p. 92. Quoted by permission.

Chapter V

PREDICAMENT AND THEME

1 This "principle of correspondence" is similar to, but not identical with, Paul Tillich's "method of correlation," as described in his *Systematic Theology* (Chicago, University of Chicago Press, 1951), I 59 ff. The similarity lies in the mutuality between revelation and human need. The difference is that "the principle of correspondence" makes the mutuality *personal* to a degree which Professor Tillich does not seem prepared to affirm. Among recent writers Herbert H. Farmer, in *God and Men* (New York, Abingdon Press, 1947), maintains that a "radical personalism" is not only characteristic of Christianity but is essential for our understanding of our world and God. Reuel Howe, in *Man's Need and God's Action* (Greenwich, The Seabury Press, 1953), has used Tillich's principle of correlation but has given it a Biblically personalistic form.

2 Cf. W. C. Bower, *The Living Bible* (New York, Harper & Brothers, 1936).

3 See, e.g., Leviticus 25.

4 Cf. Chap. II, above.

Chapter VI

Communication Through Symbols

[1] In the treatment of this section especial indebtedness is acknowledged to a paper entitled "The Individual, the Religious Community and the Symbol," prepared by John E. Smith and presented to the Thirteenth Conference on Science, Philosophy and Religion at Columbia University; and to Paul Tillich's *Systematic Theology*, Vol. I, for its references to the philosophical-theological aspects of symbols. See also *Religious Symbolism*, edited by F. Ernest Johnson (New York, Harper & Brothers, 1955). *Christian Doubt* by Geddes MacGregor (London, Longmans, Green & Co., 1952) is relevant to the relation between communication and doubt; he maintains that wonder and doubt are "Implicates" of Christian faith. Smith's paper is reproduced in *Symbols and Values: An Initial Study*, edited by Lyman Bryson and others (New York, Harper & Brothers, 1954).

[2] Exodus 12:26, 13:13 ff.; Joshua 4:6. Deuteronomy 6:20 applies the same principle to any and all statutes of the law.

[3] Exodus, Chapter 3.

[4] E.g., Philippians 2:10; Ephesians 1:21.

[5] Genesis 18:1, 2.

[6] Exodus 33:17 ff.

[7] Several instances, e.g., I Kings 8:10 ff.

[8] E.g. in Judges 2:1 ff.; 6:11 ff.

[9] As Gideon, Judges 6:24, ASV margin.

[10] Deuteronomy 26:5.

[11] Deuteronomy 6:4.

[12] John 1:4.

[13] Romans 10:17.

[14] Acts 12:24.

Chapter VII

Changes in the Self

[1] L. E. Cole and W. F. Bruce, *Educational Psychology* (New York, World Book Co., 1950), Chap. 11. Chaps. 11, 12, and 13 contain a useful summary of the work on learning.

[2] The "laws of learning" are stated in E. L. Thorndike, *Educational Psychology, II* (New York, Teachers College, Columbia University, 1913), 1–5. His "characteristics of learning" are stated in his *Educational Psychology, Briefer Course* (New York, Teachers College, Columbia University, 1914), pp. 131 ff.

3 John Dewey, *How We Think* (new ed., Boston, D. C. Heath & Co., 1933), Chap. 7.

4 Dewey, *Reconstruction in Philosophy* (enlarged edition, Boston, Beacon Press, 1949), *passim.*

5 Dewey, *Democracy and Education* (New York, The Macmillan Co., 1916).

6 See, e.g., a critique in M. R. Cohen, *Studies in Philosophy and Science* (New York, Henry Holt & Co., 1949), Bk. II, Chap. 3.

7 One may again compare Reuel Howe's *Man's Need and God's Action.*

Chapter VIII

The Dynamics of Becoming

1 P. Tillich, "Creative Love in Education," *World Christian Education*, Vol. IV, No. 2, 1949.

2 Ross Snyder, "Religious Living with Three- and Four-Year Olds," *Chicago Theological Seminary Register*, January, 1953.

3 Randolph Crump Miller, *The Clue to Christian Education* (New York, Charles Scribner's Sons, 1950).

4 Cf., e.g., H. Peterson (ed.), *Great Teachers* (New Brunswick, N.J., Rutgers University Press, 1946).

5 W. E. Oates, *The Bible in Pastoral Care* (Philadelphia, Westminster Press, 1953), Chap. 1.

6 Psalm 7:5 (ASV); 16:9, 10; 108:1.

7 Psalm 57:8.

8 Ephesians 3:20.

Index

Remembering, 74, 95 f, 180
Repentance, 56
Responsibility, 54 f
Revelation, 52, 58, 69 f, 78 f, 86 f, 92 f, 105, 177, 181
Revelation, the doctrine of, 66
Revelation and education, 65 f
Revelation, fact of, 66
Revelation, media of, 69 f
Revelation, original, 86 f, 100
Revelation, relevance of, 105
Revelation, report of, 66
Revelation, response to, 86 f, 158, 160
Rice, Otis R., 60

Saul, Leon J., 32
Self, 2, 45, 165 f
Self, changes in the. *See* Changes in the self
Self, changes in the depths of. *See* Changes in the depths of the self
Self, concepts of the, 19
Self, the existing, 25
Self, idealized image of. *See* Idealized image of self
Self, image of the. *See* Image of self
Self, marks of a, 2 f
Self, potential, 19 f
Self, real, 195 f
Self, rifts in the, 12
Self-affirmation, 28
Self-consciousness, 7, 27, 40
Self-determination, 4, 40

Self-disclosure, God's, 69, 86, 87, 100
Self-knowledge, 14 f
Self-transcendence, 9, 33, 35, 40 f, 50, 51 f
Separateness, 17 f, 23 f, 31, 120
Sign, 123 f
Sin, 114
Snyder, Ross, 180
Spirit, 11
Spirit, Holy, 87, 160, 174
Spirit, realm of, 10
Splitness, 32, 55 f
Symbols, 71, 84, 96, 123 f, 159, 183, 189

Tension, 165 f
Theme, 109 f, 174 f, 177, 183
Therapy, 31
Thorndike, Edward L., 149
Tillich, Paul, 28, 179, 198
Togetherness, 17, 23, 31
Trial and Error, 148 f

Ultimacy, principle of. *See* Principle of ultimacy

Vieth, Paul H., 198
Vitality, 2, 40
Vocation, theme of, 110, 113 f

Watson, John B., 148
Wholeness, xii, 22, 32 f
Will, ontological, 4
Will, psychological, 4 f